From Pigtails to Chin Hairs
(A Memoir and More)

by
Becky Lewellen Povich

From Pigtails to Chin Hairs

These stories are true, but they are my memories and mine alone. Many of the names are real and used with permission. Others have been changed for obvious reasons.

Permission from Hasbro: for the use of a Monopoly phrase in "Paradise on Preston Lane"

Permission from Stephanie Piro: for the use of exclusive cartoons in "Through the Years"

Some chapters of this book have appeared in complete or edited form in various print and/or internet publications, and have reprint permission. Those permission acknowledgements appear on page 298.

~~~

"If it hadn't been for my father, both literally and figuratively, this memoir would never have been written."

ISBN-13: 978-1481157490
ISBN-10: 1481157493

10 9 8 7 6 5 4

Printed in the USA

Praise for
From Pigtails to Chin Hairs:
A Memoir and More

"In Becky Povich's beguiling memoir, the title says it all: *From Pigtails to Chin Hairs: A Memoir and More*. That alone caught my attention, leading me to explore the content between the two vintage designed covers of her memoir. Once inside, the journey became personal, as I'm sure it has for an ever-growing legion of fans.

"Povich serves her readers a delectable brew as she guides them through familiar waters, distilling the essence of her life into a complex elixir flavored with a diversity of flavorings. From humorous to poignant to self-effacing, the reader will find touchstone recollections which will, in turn, spark readers to wander through their own memories. I often found myself putting Povich's book down while I stopped in my cerebral rest stop to pursue my own past, and marvel at the similarities and differences. This is not a book through which one races – savor the nuances and differences, as one savors a multi-course banquet.

"Lacking any pretentious overtones, Povich has crafted another addition to the pantheon of alluring memoirs. Honest, revealing, conspiratorial, mirthful – readers will find their own labels as they enjoy their journey through *From Pigtails to Chin Hairs: A Memoir and More*. Be sure to have your favorite comfort drink by your side – tea, coffee, lemonade – as this is as much a conversation with Becky Povich sharing her side of life, as it is a reminiscence oasis."
- John Busbee: writer and actor, also the producer and host of "The Culture Buzz" on KFMG 99.1 FM, Des Moines, Iowa.

"Funny the way life's trials and tribulations can make you laugh out loud when they're happening to Becky Povich. In her memoir, *From Pigtails to Chin Hairs*, Becky recalls a life's journey not always funny, to be sure, but told always with a wry bemusement that charms and delights. A wonderfully engaging story of the heroine next door."
- ROBERT BRAULT, Author of "Enjoy the little things, for one day you may look back and realize they were the big things." ....among thousands of others.

More Praise for
From Pigtails to Chin Hairs:
A Memoir and More

"If you wish to step back in time and enjoy memories of the period, this book is what you need. Take your time with it, though, because you don't want to read it fast. Each paragraph is a déjà vu, a throwback to a simpler time. Povich captures smells, experiences, innovations, and the way parenting used to be. Food, travel, playing outside till dinner. There's so much rich material here you can't digest it at once. Enjoyable read."

- C. HOPE CLARK, Author of the *Carolina Slade Mystery Series*, and editor of *Funds for Writers*.

"Charming." - A.E. HOTCHNER, bestselling author of *Doris Day: Her Own Story*, commenting on the chapter "Doris Day, AE Hotchner, and Me".

"*From Pigtails to Chin Hairs* is a perfect title to describe this new memoir. Becky writes from the heart and her warmth resonates throughout these essays. You are on Becky's side from page one. Her life hasn't always been easy but she manages to look for the humor in any given situation. She writes about her happy childhood growing up in a 1950's neighborhood…the kind of place where kids played games together outside or watched black and white TV with the family, a time when watching TV was an event!...She adored her handsome father… but those happy times come to an end, and Becky isn't afraid to write about her parents' divorce and the hardships that the family dealt with afterwards.

"Later on she becomes a young Army wife and mother of a young son who follows her husband to Germany. There is a lot more to Becky's story…Enjoy this wonderful memoir (it even has cartoons!)"

STEPHANIE PIRO, syndicated cartoonist and one of the Six Chix, women cartoonists whose work appears in newspapers throughout the country.

Acknowledgements

Do readers ever bother to read every word of lengthy acknowledgements? I doubt it. How many friends, family, and colleagues can an author thank, without accidentally leaving someone out, thus causing hurt feelings? I obviously must thank *some* people, so this will be as short as possible.

First and foremost, I thank my husband, Ron, who from the very beginning always believed in me. He never complained about the hours I spent on my new found passion; whether it was time devoted to actually writing and editing, or attending critique groups, or Saturday Writers meetings, or any other get-together with writer-friends. He also urged me to keep on writing and never give up when self-doubt reared its ugly head. You kept me going. You made me believe in myself.

Thank you to all other family members and writer-friends. Thank you to neighbors, non-writer friends, and church members who congratulated me on my early successes.

I also have to say thank you to two women who encouraged me many, many years ago and never doubted my ability. They thought I could write, therefore I kept writing. Karen Buss, and Angie Sendejas Lippert, I thank you both with all my heart.

And, a huge thank you to *Sistah Teri*. You, too, were always there for me!

I owe so much to Julie Failla Earhart. I'll truly be indebted to her for the rest of my writing-life! Julie gave me my first professional critique in 2007 and said, "You have talent." Thank you, Julie. You gave me the courage to believe in myself and to keep writing.

Thank you to Margo Dill for friendship and guidance, Kelly Cochran for believing I could actually create my own cover, Jennifer Hasheider for maintaining my website, and especially Brad Watson for all the hours spent formatting my manuscript and making my book cover come to life. You are one incredibly patient man. (Isn't that an oxymoron?)

A huge thank-you to all my Kickstarter supporters. Your belief in me was incredible.

Thanks to all my friends in the Tuesday C&C group, Saturday Writers, SLWG, MWG, SLPA, and all the other writers who inspired and influenced me along the way.

Thank you to two wonderful writer-friends who are no longer here on this earth, but will forever be in my heart: Bea Siros and Nick Nixon of the Tuesday Coffee & Critique group, and Saturday Writers (St. Peters, Mo). You helped me become a better writer and conceivably a better person. I miss you both every day.

Author's Notes

When I decided to write my memoir, there were no particular stories I wanted to include, other than "the crowbar incident." I wrote and rewrote that chapter a zillion times. (I may be slightly exaggerating, but not by much.) At that time, I didn't belong to any writers or critique groups, and barely knew any local writers. I'd never taken any writing classes and knew nothing about the foreign words and phrases I heard: genre, clips, protagonist, point-of-view (pov), freewriting, galleys, query, print-on-demand (pod), vanity press, etc. Somehow, though, during the next few years, I met, joined, participated, and wrote. I read books about the craft of writing, with advice from the best of the best. It began to sink in. I submitted stories to different anthologies and a couple were accepted and published. What a thrill! I also sent some to magazines, contests, and other venues, which were rejected. And, sure, that stung, but after my initial disappointment I knew rejection was okay. The editors weren't rejecting ME, just my particular story. Rejection notices at least meant I was writing and submitting. It's like the lottery: You can't win, if you don't play.

As I began to think seriously about writing my memoir, ideas began bursting in my mind like popcorn kernels. Day or night, it didn't matter when or where: While driving my car, strolling down grocery store aisles, spending time with my beloved dog, Tiger, and then after her, our new, sweet dog

Vern. Also when washing my hair, watching TV, reading a book, and sometimes even in my sleep. I kept tiny note pads and pens everywhere so I could jot down the main thought until I could get to my laptop and write at least a few sentences. Even with my seemingly organized methods, I'd still have to write on a napkin, envelope, or blank section of a newspaper every now and then. It's wonderful when those feelings and visions are there, but even better when the right words just flow from my mind and heart, through my fingertips, and onto the keyboard. Wow! If only writing was always that easy.

Words did come easily the day I sat down to write about my ailing father in May of 2001. When I got the phone call from my brother, Mike, that our dad wasn't expected to live, my husband Ron, and our youngest son Mark, and I drove immediately to Iowa. Even though I wasn't really sure how I felt, or what I'd say to Dad, I knew I had to be by his side.

The story I wrote after we came home, the one that flowed so easily, landed me a part-time spot in a local newspaper, the St. Charles County Journal. When I received the phone call from the editor, Dennis Miller, telling me I was one of the few chosen, that's when I knew I could write. The minute I hung up the phone, I jumped up from my desk chair, ran out into the upstairs hallway, and yelled, "I'm a writer! I'm a writer!" It didn't matter that it was an unpaid position for a mere five columns a year. It was a great opportunity and thrilling to see my name, my photo, and my column in the Opinion Section. (And no, the editor is not the comedian, Dennis Miller!)

It was also during that time I bought Haven Kimmel's memoir, *A Girl Named Zippy: Growing Up Small in Mooreland, Indiana.* I loved that book. It mesmerized me. It inspired me. It gave me the notion and courage to make the decision to attempt writing my own memoir.

The writer, George Eliot said, "It's never too late to be who you might have been."

So, finally, all these years later, I've done it. I've written my memoir. But, it's only the beginning. I've already begun writing a sequel, because I still have so many memories to share. Please look for it sometime during 2015.

From Pigtails to Chin Hairs

~ ~ ~

"My mother told me in so many words she thought I was nuts."

From Pigtails to Chin Hairs

From Pigtails to Chin Hairs
(A Memoir and More)

From Pigtails to Chin Hairs

Table of Contents

Mike and Becky in front of house on Preston Lane 1959.

(I remember his red barn lunch bucket and school satchel!)

Part I:

THE 1950s WERE ALMOST PERFECT

From Pigtails to Chin Hairs

Paradise on Preston Lane

While writing my memoir these past few years, I've driven down Preston Lane many times. As I inched along, trying to take in all the details on both sides of that little street in Cahokia, Illinois, I'd be back in the 1950s again. The houses didn't look much different, only smaller than I remembered. One still has those window awnings monogrammed with the letter "M" and they aren't a bit rusty. All the houses have the old, white (now yellowed) asbestos siding—except for the one red brick house where the "rich people" lived. (The dad owned a local Tom Boy grocery store.) Most still had the same, concrete front porches, having acquired a few cracks during the past decades. The yards seemed to have shrunk, especially in contrast to the trees, which appeared as tall and wide as Jack's beanstalk. The street itself was so much shorter in both length and width than I'd remembered, too.

There are about twenty small houses on that tiny dead-end street. It was my neighborhood, my family, my life— until the year we moved away when I was eight years old. Most of my recollections of those years are summertime adventures, although I have vivid Christmas memories, too. We knew all of our neighbors, and it was completely safe and normal to wander up and down our street. In fact, it's what parents wanted us kids to do. "Go outside and play!" were the most frequently spoken words by them, and that's exactly what we did.

Those were the days of imagination and make-believe. We didn't have toys to entertain us. We didn't need them. We entertained ourselves. I was quite a tomboy, too, probably because there were more boys on our street than girls. There was my brother, Mike, who is a mere 15 months older than I am. Next door were two more boys in our age group, Edwin and Earl, and another boy across the street. One little girl lived down at the end of our lane, but she didn't come outside much. Sometimes I'd go there, and we'd play House or School in her basement, where it was so much cooler, but I never stayed long because I liked the outdoors better. The only other girls were a bit older, so it was mostly me 'n' the boys. We played Cowboys & Indians, plus War, with lots of shoot-'em-up, and sometimes, we even had caps for our guns. What a treat! If the toy guns were broken, we'd get a hammer and take turns pounding strips of caps on our sidewalk, one dot at a time. It took many days for those black burn marks to wear off and sometimes they never did. I wonder if any are still faintly showing on that strip of cement!

I remember lying in the shady grass, my face about six inches above it, searching for four-leaf clovers. If I didn't find any, I picked lots of the white, flowery clover and ran inside with a fistful of them for Mother. Nobody on our street had what today would be called a "manicured lawn." On the contrary. Yards were mostly green consisting of clover, weeds, and a bit of grass. The non-green parts contained dandelions, both yellow and white, and small patches of dirt where us kids most likely pulled up grass and weeds to make a toy car driveway. Sometimes a larger dirt area was created so we could play Marbles. My favorites were the Cat's-Eyes!

I particularly loved climbing our weeping willow tree. It was in the farthest corner of the back yard and I felt completely removed from my home. In my young mind, running on my short, little legs, it seemed to be miles away. I'd climb up two or three branches and pretend to be a captain on a pirate ship. The branches and I swayed in the breezes as if my ship was rocking against some rough waves. I hung on for dear life and called out, "Ay, Matey! Bring me my spyglass and a bottle of rum!" No, I definitely was not the kidnapped maiden. I was the Captain. The funniest thing about my pirate adventures is that I was probably only about two feet from the ground!

One of my favorite outdoor games was Indian Ball, or our version of it; a game we played in the middle of our street. We usually began right after supper and we were allowed to stay out until the streetlight came on. I don't know if anyone actually knew any rules, but part of it had to do with laying the bat down on the street, and someone else trying to roll the ball and hit it. Then it was someone else's turn to bat. Even the older girls came out and joined in the fun.

Oh, how I loved to hear the song of the locusts. (I discovered a few years ago that the creatures I've known my entire life as locusts are really cicadas. But since my parents, grandparents, neighbors, and other relatives all called them locusts, and that's all I've ever known them as, I cannot call them anything different now! I read somewhere that lots of folks do refer to them that way. It depends on what part of the country people are from, I guess.)

One of the girls was Diane, the older sister of Edwin and Earl. I thought she was especially smart and pretty and loved it when she took time to hang out with us. She always had great ideas about things we could do and was always "in charge." A couple of times, we put on parades and asked all the grown-ups to come outside and watch. Sometimes we road bikes or trikes and we could make them sound like motorcycles by attaching baseball cards with our mothers' clothespins. It made amazing flapping noises against the spokes.

Other times we walked and pulled wagons, and we always had some homemade signs or banners. We honked our bike horns and/or sang songs. We practiced long and hard because we wanted our parades to be special. The adults would come out and sit on the small slabs that were the front porches, waving and clapping as we marched by. Most of them were older and didn't have kids living at home anymore, and they were so kindhearted. Most always bought our homemade, woven pot-holders, too, when we came knocking on their doors, selling them for 5 or 10 cents apiece. It was as if we were all related and had extra grandparents.

Diane also originated Court Day. A couple of us younger kids must've done or said something wrong, and there were hurt feelings. Court was held in their garage, and Diane was the judge. There were tables and chairs, a hammer used as the gavel, witnesses and pledges to tell the truth; and by the time it was all over, everyone was happy again. It sounds like a Little Rascals or Our Gang episode, doesn't it?

One other noteworthy event held in the same garage was "The Wedding" between Earl and me. My veil of toilet paper, bobby pinned to my hair, dragged along behind me. My bouquet was a handful of dandelions. I don't remember who portrayed the priest/minister, and it didn't matter that I was Catholic, and Earl was Protestant. Although millions of people cared a great deal about that in those days, thankfully none of our parents did, and they got the message across to us kids to not be prejudiced. Our friends across the street were Jewish, and that didn't matter either. After our parents explained a little about their faith to Mike and me, I felt sorry for them because they didn't get to celebrate Christmas. But that changed the day they put an aluminum tree in their picture window, complete with revolving colored lights and all.

Besides having the occasional ice cream truck come down our street, we also had "The Snow Cone Man." He was just a regular guy with an ice crusher machine, paper cones, and several bottles of flavors inside the trunk of his car. I think he just hollered out, "Snow cone man!" Since we didn't have air conditioning and our windows were always open, we knew when he was here.

Every kid on the block would run outside, slamming the screen door behind them, and buy a snow cone for just 10 cents each. My favorite was always grape. Can you imagine that happening these days? The guy would be out of business in two seconds. He'd be accused of being a child molester, be handcuffed, and taken away. "Go directly to jail. Do not pass Go. Do not collect $200.00."

Another truck we loved to see driving down our street was the mosquito spray truck. A machine in the back of it blew tons of stinky, smoky fumes up and over our entire neighborhood. We'd run behind it, waving our arms around, as if we were helping to whoosh the smoke in all the right directions. Hmmm . . . maybe that could explain a lot of things.

The memories I've kept all these years are still so vibrant and alive.

Many times I wonder why I was so fortunate to spend the first few years of my life on this tiny piece of paradise, this speck of heaven in the vast universe we call our world.

I Adored My Dad

I was born in 1953, during the Golden Age of Television. We had the typical size TV, a huge, heavy box of a thing with a small, glass front. And as far back as I remember, we had one.

Dad was the one in our family most interested in it, and he seemed to enjoy the challenge of getting the best picture. First, he'd turn on the TV, and sometimes, it made a humming noise as it warmed up; then he had to wait for the picture to appear, which took a long time. Then he'd adjust the antenna, aka rabbit ears, to try to get the best reception. If that didn't work the way it should, he'd wrap some shiny aluminum foil around the "ears." Then there were the horizontal and vertical knobs. Those were needed to fix any zig-zaggy lines that happened. The knobs were "touchy," according to Dad. If you didn't turn them just the right way and stop just the instant you should, the picture would still be messed up. (And remote control? It would be a long time before that was invented. Someone always had to get up from where they were sitting to change the channels or fix the volume.) Sometimes it was hard work getting that darned thing to behave.

He watched it almost every minute he was home, including late at night when the rest of us had gone to bed, including Mother. I guess she was a light sleeper because the sound always seemed to bother her, no matter how low Dad tried to keep it. He fixed that problem, though. Somehow he hooked up a speaker with a long cord attached to it and listened to his programs by resting it on one of his shoulders, keeping the volume way down. I'd see him once in a while when I'd wake up to use the bathroom. He looked pretty funny with that big wooden box on his shoulder next to his ear, but it worked. (I think he half-way invented the Boom Box!)

There were only a couple of times when the TV wasn't on. One would be if someone was listening to music on our hi-fi, and the other would be if a Cardinals baseball game was on the radio. It was the era of Stan "The Man" Musial and I certainly recall the voice of Harry Caray, the legendary St. Louis Cardinals radio announcer. Even as a little girl, I loved his voice, and the way he'd call a home run for our team. "It **might** be. It **could** be. It **is**! A **home run**! **Holy Cow**!"

I imagine the excitement surrounding the invention of TV was comparable to our amazement about the Internet. (Thanks once again, Mr. Gore.) Television was so different back then. There were only three or four channels and they "signed off" at midnight and "signed on" early in the morning. If the TV was turned on sometime between midnight and 6:00 am, there was nothing but a "test pattern" on it. I have no idea why it was called that. I just thought it looked like a picture of an Indian face and some circles that looked like targets. Color TV hadn't been invented yet; and when it was, it would be years before anyone in our family had one.

Some of my best memories are the times Dad and I watched TV together. It was more than just sitting, side by side, on our scratchy couch. (What *was* that material?

I loved watching him as he watched TV. It was a show all by itself, an interactive one, and I was mesmerized every time.

The TV took up quite a bit of space in our tiny living room. The rest of the area was a bit crowded with that colorless, itchy couch, a soft chair with huge, red and pink flowers, a rocker covered with bright green vinyl, a wooden coffee table, and an end table. On the coffee table was a large, glass ashtray, a pack or two of Dad's L&M cigarettes, a shiny Zippo lighter, a pile of newspapers, a cup of coffee, and sometimes an open box of sugar cubes. They weren't there to drop into his coffee, but to pop into his mouth from time to time to "help his blood sugar." I wasn't really sure what that meant, but I knew it had something to do with going to the doctor. (My doctor never told ME to eat more sugar than I already did.)

The end table held a pink lamp, with a big, white lampshade, and a really cool thing called a Silent Butler. It was about eight inches square and shiny with a lid and handle. Whoever happened to think of it, usually Mother, would carry it around the house and empty all the ashtrays into it. I don't remember who explained its use to me, but I thought it was pretty fancy.

Dad would be so busy trying to watch TV while peering over his newspaper and holding his cigarette that he'd be lost to the world. It was as if he were daydreaming. Trying to get his attention during those times was next to impossible. I would watch the long ash of his cigarette hanging on for dear life, slowly bending down farther and farther, until it was the size of a gray wooly worm. Not being able to stand it a second longer, I'd finally yell, "Dad! Your ashes are falling!" I'd usually grab the ashtray and catch them just in the nick of time. He'd nonchalantly glance my way, as if he'd forgotten I was even there. He'd let out a chuckle and thank me for being so watchful. Afterwards, he'd go back to doing it all over again.

I just adored him. He was a teacher at a nearby college, and I thought he was the smartest, handsomest dad on our street. He could've been a movie star or one of the actors in the TV westerns we watched together. I knew handsome when I saw it, even at the young age of five or six. I was in love with Rowdy Yates (Clint Eastwood) and Mr. Favor on Rawhide, plus Bret Maverick (James Garner) and all three of the sons on Bonanza—even Hoss. He was the sweetest, most lovable of them all, and I found that so appealing.

Since there were only a few channels to watch, it was common to walk down the street and hear the exact same program in all the houses: The Ed Sullivan Show, Lawrence Welk, Gunsmoke. No air conditioning, windows wide open, I not only liked to hear what shows my neighbors watched, but also listen to any conversations that were going on. For some reason I found that comforting.

Dad had a great sense of humor, and his laugh is another fond memory of mine. Sometimes he'd watch Saturday morning TV with Mike and me. He really got a kick out of Yogi Bear, Huckleberry Hound, The Road Runner, and others. I thought it was neat that a dad liked cartoons. As I grew up, though, I realized lots of the dialogue was really geared toward adults, and most of the humor went right over kids' heads. When The Flintstones premiered in 1960, being the first primetime animated show, you can bet our TV was tuned to that channel. It became another favorite of Dad's, too.

Those special times were cut short when my parents divorced a few years later, and Dad lived hundreds of miles away. Thus began 40 plus years of an estranged relationship with him—one that lasted almost until his death in 2002.

From Pigtails to Chin Hairs

The Little Train that Couldn't

I have only a handful of memories from my first couple of years of grade school, and two of them are from first grade. One is during my first day, trying to eat my sack lunch at my brand new desk in a brand new school. We had milk that came in little glass bottles, and I'm sure at least one kid spilled or broke theirs. I started crying at lunch time, too, wanting to go home because I missed my mother. (We didn't have kindergarten at my school, and with the birthday cut-off date, I was close to seven years old when I went. I guess being home with Mother every day for that many years made it harder on me.)

The nuns brought my brother in from his third grade classroom to try to calm me down. I guess it worked because I managed to make it through that first scary day, and the rest of the year.

Another memorable incident happened a few months later in the girl's lavatory. I had to go Number Two, and after receiving permission to leave class, I meandered on down the hall. I was thankful it was empty, so I would be alone; but after sitting down in one of the stalls, nothing happened. For a long, long time, nothing happened. Being a six- year-old girl who always looked for approval both at home and at school, I didn't know what to do. I was positive that if I stayed long enough, trying as hard as I could, I would get the job done. I was afraid if I gave up too soon, I'd just have to ask to come back again; and I might not get permission a second time. And some of the other kids might think I was weird and laugh at me.

So, I made the decision to stay a while longer. As I sat, I began to worry. What if I'm *never* able to *go* again? Even though I knew nothing about the workings of the human body, somehow I was positive that would be a very bad thing. What if I get in trouble when I finally get out of here? Will my teacher, or worse yet the principal, call my mother and say I'm expelled for spending too much time in the girls bathroom? The more worried I got, the worse my predicament became. I became immovable, in more ways than one.

After thinking about every rule I might be breaking, I began to cry. I wondered why there hadn't been any other students come in, either. Part of me didn't want anyone else to come in since I was embarrassed about being there so long, but the other part of me was worried that I'd be stuck in here forever because nobody came in.

Just about that same time, Sister must've finally decided to have one of my classmates check on me. Someone pushed open the huge door and yelled, "Becky?"

"I'm in here!" I called back.

I heard shoes scuff across the tile floor, as she walked over to my stall. I saw her Mary Jane shoes, as she stopped in front of my closed door,

"Sister Theresa sent me to look for you. It's me, Claudette. Are you all right?"

"I don't know," I sniffed. "I'm having trouble going . . . you know . . . Number Two."

"Oh, that happens to me a lot," she said.

"Really?" Thank God I wasn't the only one, and that there wasn't anything wrong with me! "What do you do when you get ... stuck?"

"Oh, that's easy," she declared. "I just think to myself about the story of that little train. You know the one that says, 'I think I can. I think I can. I *know* I can.' I just keep repeating that over and over in my head, and then it works!"

Hmmm, well since nothing else had worked at that point, I decided to give it a try. I told her to go on back to the classroom and let Sister Theresa know I was okay and that I'd be back soon. A few minutes later—success!

When I think back on that episode, I certainly laugh about it. I've always been grateful to the little girl who had the compassion to help a classmate she really didn't know very well. And especially, one who had a predicament nobody wants to find themselves in. Thank goodness for Claudette, the Little Engine Who Could.

From Pigtails to Chin Hairs

Multiplication Made Easy

Most of my life, I've been a naïve, trusting soul—sometimes to the point of being laughed at, but usually in a gentle way. You'd think that after so many years of realizing things weren't the way they appeared, I'd be more astute. I guess I'm a little better at it now, but looking back . . .

It was during second grade at St. Catherine Laboure School, in Cahokia, Illinois. Our class was learning the times tables. I easily memorized the lower numbers: 2 x 1 = 2, 3 x 1 = 3, etc.; but when we got to those higher numbers, I began to have trouble. Who the heck could learn and remember problems like 9 x 12 = 108?

One day during recess, I overheard a girl I didn't know talking about how a kid she knew was able to cheat on a test. She didn't get caught, and besides, it wasn't really cheating! Well, I had to hear more about that. She said a friend of hers, Sally, had a really messy desk with papers sticking out everywhere. Some were all wrinkled or wadded up, but others were flat and stuck out through slits on the side. (Our desks were the kind where everything was stored underneath our seat. We had to bend over to the left side and view everything upside down to find what we needed.)

She continued, "So when Sally dropped her pencil and leaned to the right to find it, she saw her spelling words paper hanging out through one of those little cracks. During the test, she just leaned over a little, looked down, and saw the words. She just copied them onto her paper."

Hmmm, so that wasn't cheating, huh? Maybe something like that could help me with my times tables. We were having a test on the "nines" in a couple of days; but I wasn't a messy person, and I didn't want papers hanging out of my desk either. The idea came to me to have all the answers on a piece of paper and just put it in the back of my tablet. As my teacher, Miss Mary Ann, called out each question, I nonchalantly flipped open the notepad, found the answer, and wrote it on the test paper. (Here's the kicker to my stupidity in all this: I sat in the front row just a few feet away from Miss Mary Ann.)

While I mentally patted myself on my back for being so smart, she saw every move I made. I thought I'd gotten an A on my test and that the note she gave me to take home to my parents was to share the exciting news.

When I jumped off the school bus that afternoon, I had no idea what was to come. I turned to wave good-bye to my friends and then skipped along the street to my house. As I swung my satchel, my navy blue uniform jumper swished back and forth, and I hadn't a care in the world. Until that is, I gave my mother the note. Her face went from smiling and happy to anger and disappointment. I may have even gotten a swat or two on my bottom, but I particularly remember her expression, and that is what hurt me the most.

"Do you know what this note says?" she asked.

I already knew it wasn't something good from her face and her tone. "No, ma'am."

"Miss Mary Ann says you **cheated** during the times table test today! Rebecca Anne, is that right? Did you *cheat*?"

Oh my gosh. I know I'm in big trouble when I'm called Rebecca!

"Uh…well, I uh—"

"I can't believe this! You know better than to do something like this. You know it's wrong to cheat. And it's a *sin*!"

There it was—the dreaded guilt of sin being laid on me. I'd never seen my mother so upset, about *anyone* or *anything*, and here she was angry with *me*. I guess I was going to go to Hell. Attending a Catholic school Monday through Friday and Mass every Sunday, I knew all about Heaven and Hell and sins. But what I did should only be a venial sin, shouldn't it? Not the horrible, mortal kind.

I started to explain about the paper hanging out of someone's desk, and how I thought I could do something like that, too, and how it wasn't really cheating. But when I stopped to take a breath, I knew it was useless, and she said, "We'll talk to your daddy about this when he gets home. I'm sure he'll be very sad, too, when he hears what you've done."

My actual punishment was writing all the multiplication tables about a zillion times. I had to do them every afternoon the minute I got home from school, and I couldn't watch my TV shows either, until I finished. But my real punishment was the disappointment I caused my parents, my teacher, and myself. I never wanted them to feel that way again because of something I did, or didn't do. I'm really glad it happened early in my life. It made me learn those darn times tables. It taught me about embarrassment, anger, hurt, and forgiveness. And I never cheated again.

Although I haven't been consumed with guilt about it all these years, it does pop into my mind every now and then. I always laugh at that little inner girl who thought she could get away with something so outrageous. Thank goodness I got caught and had the kind of parents I had. Otherwise, who knows? I may have turned into a hardened criminal.

The 1950s Were Almost Perfect

As I approached the age of 50, I started to look more like my mother. You know that light bulb moment when you look in the mirror and all of a sudden you see it—your mother's face staring back at you. I don't particularly favor her that much. It's more of a facial expression and gesture kind of thing. And now that I'm 60, I've definitely inherited her saggy double chin and her flabby upper arms—two things I used to make fun of when I was younger. Payback is hell.

Mother was a true homemaker, in the 1950s kind of way, and I believe she was very happy in those days. She baked homemade bread and cinnamon rolls and cooked large meals for supper, like pot roast, fried chicken, potatoes, and corn on the cob. You name it. She baked special cakes on Easter and our birthdays and wonderful cookies at Christmas. She let me watch and also showed me things I could do to help, like using the cookie cutter; plus she let me lick cake batter and frosting off the spatula. If Mike was home at the same time, we had to share, but that was okay, too.

I also liked to amuse myself exploring the things she kept on top of the bedroom chest of drawers in her and Dad's bedroom. Good thing it wasn't very high or else I wouldn't have been able to see anything. My chin could just about rest on it; so every time I wanted to look at something really good, I had to reach and pull it towards me. For some reason, I was captivated by a small, decorative, cardboard box she kept hankies and a necklace of pink beads in. I thought they were so pretty and I don't think I ever missed the opportunity to gently lift them out and put them around my neck. I had to admire myself in Mother's hand mirror since I was too short to see myself in the one on the wall over the dresser. Even though it was light as a shoebox, it seemed so elegant to me, and I couldn't help but daydream about its beauty and where it came from.

Mother's jewelry box was nothing fancy, just the typical one of the era; but when I opened it and peered inside, I saw elegance. She had bracelets, rings, brooches, earrings, and more necklaces, too. Every pair of her earrings were the screw-on type, and trying them on was usually a big mistake. I'd turn the tiny screw too many times, and it would hurt so bad I'd scream. I couldn't yank it off without tearing a big chunk of my earlobe along with it, so thank goodness Mother always came to my rescue. And yes, I usually had to endure one of her "reminders" about not doing that again. It didn't seem to stop me though.

The dresser also had a bottle of coffee-colored, really stinky perfume, a statue of the Virgin Mary, and a bottle of Jergens hand lotion. The scent of

Jergens is one of *the* most powerful aromas of my memories. After all this time, whenever I smell it, my eyes close in that slow memory-flooding way and I'm surrounded by feelings of home, happiness, and childhood. For many years the original scent was either nonexistent or impossible to find, but I'm so happy it's back on the market, and I use it every day.

My dad's side of the dresser had a bottle of Old Spice and a little wooden dish that held his watch, keys, dimes, and nickels. Also, sometimes his Catholic medal of the Sacred Heart was laying in it, which he hardly ever took off. It was like dog tags. He showered with it on and slept with it on—almost always.

A year or so before I started school, I loved watching the morning kids' TV shows. One of my favorites was *Captain Kangaroo*. The entire show kept my interest and I especially liked Mr. Green Jeans and Bunny Rabbit. Another favorite was *Romper Room*, but soon I thought it was too babyish for me. In the afternoons, Mike and I both watched *Cookie and the Captain*, and *The Wrangler's Club*. They were two local shows that were very popular during the 1950s and '60s. Both shows had costumed hosts and showed cartoons.

I also watched some daytime TV with my mother. (What can I say? It was the Golden Age of Television!) *Queen for a Day* was one of our favorites. We'd listen to sad stories about some women on the show, and the one with the worst life would be crowned queen for the day. The man in charge would put a crown on her head and a cape around her, like she was a real queen. Then somebody would announce all the prizes she won, usually appliances, I think. People in the audience would be crying, while Mother and I sniffled sometimes, too.

We also watched and exercised along with Jack LaLanne. Even at five years old, I could tell that he wore weird clothes for a man—tight, stretchy pants and ballet-like shoes. Mother would pull a kitchen chair into the living room because sometimes she had to lean on it or put her leg up on it. Other times we both lay on the floor, side by side, and did sit-ups or leg lifts together.

I don't remember what brand of vacuum cleaner we had, but it was a canister type and I'm sure it wasn't one of the fancy, expensive ones. I loved watching Mother empty the bag of dirt. There weren't disposable bags then, so you didn't just take out the paper bag and toss it into the trash. The cleaner had a heavy-duty cloth bag and when it was full, Mother grabbed some old newspapers and spread them on the hardwood floor. Then she'd unlatch the bag and somehow turn it upside down onto the papers without making a big mess. Then came the fun part! She'd stand over the bag and place both feet on opposite sides, stepping onto a tiny edge that stuck out. That was the most important part because that's what kept the bag in one place. Then she'd bend over and start flapping and shaking that bag with gusto, while her two feet held it tightly down. It always made me laugh because it reminded me of the way a dog looked when he played tug-of-war. His head would shake back and forth that same way! After all the dirt was out of the bag and onto the newspapers, she wadded it all up, threw it away, and continued with the vacuuming.

Mother really liked a local variety program, *The Charlotte Peters Show*. Ms. Peters sang and interviewed many people—some famous celebrities. Even though we watched it every day, about all I remember was her theme song, "Anything Goes."

I never knew about soap operas until being in a neighbor's house one day. Mother and I walked down our street to borrow a cup of sugar. While the two ladies chatted, I looked at the TV set and heard a man's voice say something about *The Edge of Night*. It sounded really dramatic, and I wondered what happened on that particular show. After we got back home, I returned to my coloring book, and Mother went into the kitchen. I asked about the show and why we didn't watch it. She replied saying something about how she didn't like those programs, and I could tell by the tone of her voice that she disapproved of them. A few years later, I learned it was because of all the extramarital affairs that always happened on them. She had no empathy then or through the rest of her life for people she considered "immoral or guilty of *any* sins," even those on fictional programs.

As I've said before, I couldn't have been happier. I thought our family was perfect, just like *Father Knows Best*. I always thought my older sister, Marian, looked so much like Betty (Princess), the pretty older sister on the show, and I was Kathy (Kitten). Mike was too young to be Bud, and there wasn't a fourth sibling on the show for my oldest sister, Jo Ann, to be, but it still worked in my mind. Dad never cussed, either; at least not in front of us kids. The worst I ever heard him say was, "What the devil…?"

Those carefree days came to a sudden end when my dad decided he wanted a divorce, something I didn't understand at all. It was a huge shock to my brother and me. We never saw or heard our parents argue; there were never any heated discussions. In fact, they easily showed affection for each other, like sharing a hug and kiss in the kitchen. Sometimes I'd see Dad give Mother a soft swat on her butt after they kissed. I saw smiles and heard laughter. I never saw frowns or heard angry words.

They were both recent Catholic converts. Dad was first interested in learning more about the religion. He studied and then taught at Parks College, part of St. Louis University, and observed so many things. Mike and I were baptized as babies. We went to a Catholic grade school. We attended Mass every Sunday as a family. I remember one particular instance where we all knelt in a circle on our living room hardwood floor, saying the Rosary. I've never been able to understand how a man who had such a strong faith and seemed so happy, could in a few short years want out of the life he'd been living.

Mother had already endured the loss of one husband. Her first husband, George, was killed in World War II, and then her second one decided he didn't want to be married to her anymore. I know she was devastated by both losses, but probably more so by my dad because he chose to leave her.

28

The divorce was very hard on her, and I know she never really got over it. I remember feeling so bad because I couldn't do or say anything that would make her happy again, although I tried. It was quite a burden for a young girl to carry.

I learned about hardships; I watched her get a job and go to work every day, even though I knew she didn't want to. Thank goodness Jo Ann lived with us for a few years after the divorce. She helped Mother with the rent and utilities, and together, they kept us in food and clothes even on a tight budget. There never was much money left over for any "extras," and sometimes I did feel deprived.

Looking back though, I know everything that happened in my life has made me who I am today. I find happiness everywhere I go. I have a great sense of humor and I love to sing and dance and act goofy. I appreciate the smallest gifts that life has to offer. I know having Jo Ann in my life at that time has so much to do with my adult personality. I probably would've become a worried, depressed, unhappy woman just like Mother if it hadn't been for her. I think she put her life on hold during those years until Mike and I were in our late teens. Then she made one of her lifelong dreams come true. She packed up her clothes, the hi-fi, and a few incidentals and drove herself to Florida to begin a new era. I'll always be thankful for those years she lived with us.

From Pigtails to Chin Hairs

Did You Hear the One About A Dentist, A Priest, & Me?

When I was a little girl, I was afraid of a few things, as most children are. For me, it was dogs, the dark, and the dentist. Two out of three were fairly easy to control. Stay away from dogs and try to stay out of the dark. Now, number three was something else. It seemed my parents thought it necessary for their children to get proper dental care, even if it caused severe trauma to one of them. Me.

Our family dentist, Dr. Zimmerman, was a kind and wonderful man. He was about as calm and relaxed as anyone I'd ever seen. He spoke gently and walked leisurely, always chewing gum. (Gum? I'm pretty sure there wasn't any sugar-free gum in the 1950s.) Yet, I was terrified. I wasn't afraid of *him;* it was that huge dental chair and all those scary-looking tools on the tray: pliers, needles, and drills. Oh my! Even if he tricked me into sitting down, this little five-year-old girl was ***not*** going to open her mouth.

After a couple of appointments, which consisted of pleading, crying, yelling, and screaming (coming from me, not the dentist!), my poor exasperated mother threatened me one day with a whipping. I knew I was in big trouble when those rarely spoken words, "I'm going to go get a switch from a tree," flew out of her mouth. My parents never spanked us kids. They didn't believe in it, I guess—plus the fact we were usually good. When the few times occurred we didn't feel like doing what we were told and talking to us didn't seem to do the trick, the threat of a spanking always worked.

I clearly remember that afternoon I crossed the line with my hysterics and drove my mother to the end of her rope. She stated the dreaded "switch from the tree" threat and out the door she went, marching straight toward a small tree in the dentist's yard. Dr. Zimmerman trailed behind and managed to reason with her. "Now, Mrs. Lewellen, don't go getting your blood pressure up. Becky's young and . . ."

I couldn't hear what else was said because they were too far away. I should've realized right then and there what a wonderful dentist he was, rushing to my rescue like that. Yeah, I really should have.

~ ~ ~

My parents were friends with a priest, Father Higgins, who was an associate of my dad's at Parks College. He was also a master of hypnosis and had album recordings. My dad must've had a conversation with him about my so-called irrational fear of the dentist, because the next thing I knew, he was having supper at our house. After the normal grown-up talk, he began to ask me questions.

"Do you like to watch cartoons on TV, Becky?"

"Uh yes, sir, Father." I stirred my mashed potatoes around and kept my eyes down.

"I thought you did. How about telling me the names of some of them?"

"Umm, let me think. *Mighty Mouse, Tom & Jerry, Bugs Bunny*, and . . . and *Huckleberry Hound*."

"Oh. Those sound like great ones! Are they funny? Do they make you laugh?"

"Yes, Father." That was all he was getting out of me. I couldn't imagine why he would care about cartoons, maybe it was because my dad liked to watch them sometimes, too.

He went back to talking with my mother and dad, and I focused on the food on my plate—homemade mashed potatoes and meatloaf. Mmm! Everything seemed fine until we ate our dessert, and supper was officially over. The next thing I knew, I was sitting in the upholstered vinyl green rocking chair in our living room. Mother and Dad sat on the couch facing me, with strange looks on their faces, and Father Higgins stood next to the rocker, hovering over me. Something was up; and whatever it was, I didn't like it.

He began to speak softly about helping me get rid of my fear of the dentist. Hypnosis was explained in a way a five-year-old's mind could understand, with my parents nodding their heads in approval. Have I mentioned yet that I was a very hardheaded and determined little girl when it came to certain things? In fact—most things. I may have been afraid of going to the dentist, but I also knew there was no way in heck I was going to allow myself to be hypnotized.

He began by telling me to close my eyes and relax. *Okay, I'll play along.* Then he said, "Think about your favorite cartoon character, Huckleberry Hound, and try to breathe slowly." *Huh? I never said he was my favorite! This is stupid. I am NOT getting hypnotized!*

I almost felt sorry for Father. The more he tried, the more I resisted. I don't know how long he kept at it before he finally gave up. He pulled a hanky out of his pocket and wiped his forehead with it. He was a beaten man. Ha! I'd won!

~ ~ ~

Well, I won the battle; but as the saying goes, I lost the war. Since the hypnosis idea failed, the next trip to Dr. Zimmerman went pretty much the same as always. Only this time, the kindhearted man recommended a pediatric dentist in St. Louis he'd heard of, Dr. Smith, who was supposedly great with kids. He wrote down the phone number on a piece of paper and handed it to Mother. She apologized once again for my behavior and promised to make an appointment right away.

After she got into her side of the car and I'd climbed up into mine, she looked over at me and said,

"Becky, I hope going to this new dentist will help."

"Me too. I'm sorry for the way I acted. I just get so scared. I promise to be better next time."

Little did either of us know that "next time," which was at Dr. Smith's office, would be one of the scariest days of my life.

Scary, Dark, and Dingy

When the attempt to hypnotize me concerning my terror of dentists didn't work, Mother made an appointment with the honored Dr. Smith. What happened that day has stayed with me for over 50 years. I noticed the differences right away between the two offices. Dr. Zimmerman's was new, clean, cheerful and in a small town. Dr. Smith's was old, dark, dingy and in downtown St. Louis. The waiting room contained no toys, although it was a children's dental office. There was only a small box of trinkets that each child was allowed to choose from, *after* his or her appointment.

Parents were not allowed to go into the examining rooms with their children. That made me even more scared right off the bat. When the nurse called my name, I reluctantly got up from the chair next to my mother and walked through the door.

After the nurse put the little paper bib around my neck, I leaned back in the chair and waited for the dentist to come in. I began to cry softly as the fear crept back. I clearly remember the young nurse's pretty face as she handed me some tissues and tried to hush me and calm me down. She said

Dr. Smith would be angry if I cried, and looked as afraid of the dentist as I was. As soon as he walked in, I panicked and I must have cried louder. In my youthful eyes, he seemed huge, and he was gruff and mean-looking. As I cried harder, he pressed one of his hands over my mouth and told me to shut up and stop crying. I wanted to get out of there as fast as I could, so I did what I was told. I don't remember anything else about the actual dental exam. What I do remember is choosing a little 10 cent toy from the prize box, as my mother paid the bill. It was one of those teeny metal clicky frogs that made noise.

I was so traumatized by the actions of Dr. Smith that I know I never told Mother or anyone else. He may have even threatened me about saying anything. I've obviously forgotten most of what took place that day. I do know that I said I'd rather go back to Dr. Zimmerman because he was nicer. I promised to be good and let him work on my teeth until the day he got old and retired. I would have, too, except we moved away soon after that.

Mother Knew There Was No Santa, in More Ways than One

My brother and I never believed in Santa Claus. Why, you may ask? Our mother didn't want us to! She said when she learned the truth as a little girl she was so devastated she didn't want her own children to ever suffer the way she did. *Huh?!*

What's really strange is that I never felt as if I missed out on any Christmas fun. I didn't look at other kids and think how lucky they were because they believed in Santa, or how silly they were for believing all that hooey either.

I watched my older sisters Marian and Jo Ann wrap presents, as they sat on the twin beds in the tiny room they shared when they were younger. Marian was 14 years older than me, and Jo Ann was 16 years older. By the time I was only three years old, they were out of high school. They both attended Webster College in St. Louis, and lived in the dorms. It was founded by the Sisters of Loretto and was progressive for its time, providing higher education for women.

It wasn't very far away, so they came home occasionally on weekends. I think Marian came home more often, because her high school boyfriend continued as her college boyfriend and he lived near us. I loved my sisters so much, and I was always excited when they were around. Both of their beds were always perfectly made with pink chenille bedspreads pulled up and over the pillows all nice and neat. Wrapping paper, ribbon, gift boxes, scissors, and tape were strewn all over. My favorite wrapped presents were the ones covered in bright and shiny foil, topped with one of Jo Ann's beautifully created bows. The spools of one-inch ribbon came with "how to" directions and drawings. Artistic sister Jo Ann snipped, trimmed, tied, and taped bows on top of every gift she wrapped. Everyone agreed her packages were prettier than any magazine pictures. I was so proud of her and happy to have such a talented big sister. She majored in Art, and she could draw, paint, sketch, and sculpt. Of course, Marian's packages were pretty, too, but her main interest was Home Economics because she wanted to be a housewife. She only needed to learn how to cook, bake, clean house, sew, do laundry, and take care of her husband and kids. She didn't *need* to be artistic to do *that!*

Marian married her high school sweetheart, Kenny, right after she graduated from Webster. Mike was the ring bearer, and I was the flower girl. Marian bought fabric for my dress that matched the bridesmaids', and she sewed it herself. I had many "fittings", standing on a little stool while she pinned my dress here and there. I wasn't one to stand still for very long, but I sure was excited about being in my sister's wedding. (Already her Home Ec. classes paid off. She could sew like a skilled seamstress!) All I remember about her wedding is that I was shy about scattering the flower petals on the church floor. I did it as if I were committing a crime, sneaking one petal at a time from my tiny basket and dropping it, hoping no one would notice. During the ceremony, on the opposite side of the altar from where I stood, poor Mike cried the entire time, thinking he wouldn't see Marian anymore. He sure cried quietly because I never heard him. I only learned of it sometime later.

Those early Christmases were perfect, and I still carry them in my heart. Our tiny house didn't overflow with gifts or decorations—but with our family's love. There was a warmth to our home that even as a little girl of three or four years old I felt.

Marian and Jo Ann sang really beautifully together. They taught us many Christmas carols and "Oh, Holy Night" was one of my favorites. Of course, I also loved to sing "Rudolph the Red-Nosed Reindeer," and "Santa Claus is Coming to Town."

We had a simple balsam Christmas tree that was decorated with the same ornaments year after year, unless there was a new handmade one. Jo Ann and Marian were both very particular about putting the tinsel (or as we said: icicles) on it *carefully*—like one thin strand at a time. I'm pretty sure they let Mike and me decorate the back of the tree, which was against the wall and never seen.

Some years we had Snow-in-a-Can, and Dad sprayed that fake stuff all over the tree. I actually have a few delicate ornaments with that gunk still on them. I wonder what the heck it was made of, probably something toxic. Oh, and of course, bubble lights! The wonder of all Christmas wonders, in my opinion. I'm not sure what made them so magical to me. Maybe it was the fact that they "did" something. They "performed" for us! The other lights were pretty and colorful, too, but they just rested on the branches. Okay, I loved them both, but especially the bubble lights. And of course, as soon as presents were wrapped, they were placed under the tree to tempt everyone. (No Santa, remember?) We didn't get expensive, elaborate gifts, but we were all happy with what we received.

Mother baked all kinds of yummy goodies: Christmas cookies, cakes, sweet breads. I especially remember one fancy bread she made. She placed different lengths of rolled dough on a cookie sheet, starting with a long piece, and then smaller ones, that came out looking like a Christmas tree lying down. After it baked, she frosted it and put sprinkles all over it, which made it delicious *and* beautiful.

She always let me help in whatever way I was capable, and the aromas made everything irresistible. Helping cut out cookies was my favorite part. (I still have some of Mother's old metal cookie cutters: a Christmas tree, a bell, a Santa with a sack on his back, and a star. I love to use them in that bittersweet kind of way—part of me is happy because I'm reliving some of my youngest, happiest times and part of me is sad for the same reasons, because those days are long gone, my mother is gone, and I'm the one getting older.)

I'm so thankful for those early memories, though. They are mine, and they are precious. So many adults didn't have anything close to a happy childhood or even fragments of one.

Santa or not, those Christmases were enchanted.

~ ~ ~

After experiencing all these years of various emotions about my mother, I've come to the conclusion that although I loved her, I didn't really know her, and I resented her. When Dad left her, he left all of us, and we weren't a family who talked very much about our feelings. I couldn't discuss the sadness and gloom that surrounded us because Mother didn't want to talk about it.

Looking back, I realize I walked on eggshells for years, especially during Christmas time, attempting to do as much as I could to ease Mother's visible heartache. It was quite a burden for a young girl. We owned one Christmas album, Bing Crosby's "White Christmas," which I'd always loved. Christmas just wouldn't be the same without listening to it, even if it did remind me of my absent father. But after the first time I played it when Mother was home and saw how she fell apart during a particular song, I devised a plan. Having memorized both sides of the LP, I knew exactly when "I'll Be Home for Christmas" was going to play. So, right as "Faith of Our Fathers" was concluding, I'd jump up from where I was, run over to the hi-fi, and lift the arm mere seconds before it began. Since it was the last song on side one, I'd either place the needle back at the beginning or flip it over to side two. Like I said, I only did that when Mother was home from work or on the weekends. I could play it to my heart's desire when I got home from school every day. Did that song ever make me sad? Of course. Did I ever cry? Sure, sometimes. I also daydreamed about Dad coming back some day during the holiday season, like in a movie. I write about that in a later chapter.

I knew that never would really happen, but it was nice to imagine. And since I didn't want the "happiest time of the year" to become dreary and depressing in *my* life, I chose to be as happy and cheerful as I could, which wasn't easy at times because of Mother's depression.

Moving to Lincoln, Nebraska

Mother and Dad made moving to Lincoln, Nebraska sound like going to Disneyland. They gave Mike and me the old "Oh, you'll love it there" routine. "The house is so nice. It's going to be so much fun! You'll make new friends." Blah, blah, blah.

Dad decided he didn't want to be a teacher any longer, partly because he said he didn't really enjoy teaching and he also wanted to make more money. He accepted a job to work on an ATLAS missile underground "silo," where he was an engineering inspector. The site was near Crete, Nebraska, about 25 miles from Lincoln. If I ever did know the name of the company, I have since forgotten.

It was the summer of 1961. About all I remember is I'd just completed second grade and Mike finished the fourth. I guess I was happy and excited about moving. Marian was married, and it felt like she already lived far from us. Jo Ann transferred from Webster College a couple of times and it seemed like we barely saw her. I don't recall feeling sad about leaving our Preston Lane friends, but how could I not? I guess the most important thing to me was being with my mother, my dad, and my brother, Mike.

Things I remember seeing:

The huge, yellow/orange Allied moving van parked in front of our tiny house, taking up half the length and width of our street.

Strong-looking moving men, carrying furniture through our front door, down the porch steps and up the ramp into the truck.

Men also packing our dishes, towels, pots, and pans. Sturdy, brown cardboard boxes carried our paper-wrapped breakables.

Each box had important information printed on it with a black marker: "Kitchen-Glasses-Fragile, for example, or "Linen Closet-Towels."

We only lived in Lincoln a little over a year. I recall being happy there. I liked my school, had a best friend, Monica, who I spent lots of time with, and was excited about taking French lessons. Marian was thrilled my third grade class offered it because she had taken French in college, and I guess she hoped that someday we'd converse that way together. That never happened, though.

My birthday is in the first week of January, so sometimes I felt a bit let down about it. Often I'd be told, "This gift is for both Christmas and your birthday!" What kid ever wants to hear that?

I was not a spoiled child and certainly did not get everything I ever wanted, not by a long shot. But it was while living in Lincoln that I had a couple of disappointments when it came to gifts: that Christmas I desperately wanted an Easy Bake Oven. It was the most popular gift for girls at that time, and

I wanted one sooooo bad. *Well,* I not only didn't get one, but I got something else that felt like a slap in the face: a box of tiny cake mixes that your mother had to bake in *her* oven for you. I made one, Mother baked it, and it tasted like cardboard. Can you say "disappointed?"

The other one was when I got my first (and only) Barbie doll. She came in the package with her striped black and white swimming suit on. I don't remember if another outfit came with it or not, but I do know that I wanted lots of outfits, like my next door neighbor friends had. Mother told me we couldn't afford to buy any more and that I'd have to save my allowance. *Well,* I showed her. I took that Barbie back to the store and exchanged it for a board game, Video Village. I never did really pine for another Barbie, and I had tons of fun playing that game. (Have I mentioned I was a strong-minded little girl?)

A couple of years later I got a Tammy doll complete with a beautiful custom-made wardrobe, sewn by my big sister, Marian. (Again, those Home-Ec classes paid off!) Tammy had a cute face and a normal figure for a young girl, not at all like the busty Barbie. (Another thing my mother apparently didn't approve of.) I became an aunt when I was eight years old. Marian named her first child, a girl, Tammy. I gave my doll and clothes to her and her younger sister, Renee, a few years later when I decided I was too old for dolls.

From Pigtails to Chin Hairs

On to Tulsa, Oklahoma

We only lived in Lincoln a little over a year and then moved to Tulsa, Oklahoma. I liked Lincoln and wasn't excited about another move. I think it was because Dad was going to make more money, again, but I really don't remember. Mike and I had already begun the new school year (he was in the 6th grade and I was in the 4th) so the move was harder on us this time. I don't know how well Mike did, but I was miserable. I hated the school. Kids were "mean" and the teachers weren't much better. I faked being sick countless times so I could stay home. I know Mother saw right through me, but she felt sorry for me since she was miserable as well. I would snuggle under the covers and sleep until she brought in the-usual-stay-home-from-school-snack: cinnamon toast!

It became obvious that Mother and Dad were not happily married anymore, although they probably thought they were hiding it from us kids. That Christmas, they didn't give each other any gifts, and made up some kind of excuse about it.

Another "etched in memory" incident happened one night at the supper table when Dad began raising his voice and called Mother "stupid." She started to cry and left the table, while Mike and I just sat there dumbfounded, staring at our dad. He made some kind of remark as if to say, *What's the matter with her?* I got up from my chair and went to sit with her in their bedroom, but I don't remember what she may have said.

Other than those memories, our lives in Tulsa are still nothing more than a blur to me. Mother, Mike, and I only lived in Tulsa a month, because Mother and Dad separated. Dad stayed there, and she moved us to East St. Louis, Illinois, to be near….guess who? Marian and Jo Ann, who just happened to live a couple of blocks from each other. Marian, Kenny, and their baby, Tammy, lived in a small apartment up the hill from the tiny, one bedroom apartment Jo Ann lived in. We certainly were near Marian and Kenny, but we moved right in with Jo Ann. Talk about living in cramped quarters. We lived in that apartment for at least two years until I found out about an affordable, 3-bedroom house that was for rent. Oh, happy day!

Back When Dad Liked Me

I thought my dad only liked me when I was a little girl, still cute and tiny. You know, the young kids who say funny, entertaining things and make people laugh. He liked taking my brother and me to the aeronautical college where he taught. Mike is 15 months older than me, and I must say we were pretty darn cute.

I have a vivid memory of a particular visit to his office. I was probably five or six years old. As a child, things always look much bigger than they really are. I thought our front yard and the trees in it were huge. I even thought our living room was large, but it was barely the size of today's entry foyers. Anyway, even in my eyes, his office was really small, and he shared it with another professor. While dad worked away, sitting at his desk, I piddled around looking at pictures on the walls, diplomas, and model airplanes on book shelves. I couldn't help but notice the other teacher's messy desk. It didn't just have a few stacks of things, like my dad's. It was the biggest pile of papers and junk I'd ever seen. Mostly, there were all kinds of papers with scribbles all over them, books, pens and pencils, and a large ashtray overflowing with cigarette stubs and ashes. It wasn't just a messy pile. It was a mountain. That poor man needed help, and I decided right then and there I would straighten it up for him. My dad had a way of tuning out us kids when he focused on something like his favorite TV show, or the newspaper he was reading; so I don't know if he really didn't realize what I was doing just two feet away from him or if he thought it would be funny when the other guy got back from vacation.

I began to grab papers, shake and shuffle them until they were in neat little groups and then stacked them in piles on the desk top. Pencils were sharpened and placed in a coffee cup along with his pens. I also emptied the ashtray and tried to dust a little bit with a Kleenex. I was so pleased with myself. I'd stayed out of Dad's way and did something really nice for someone at the same time. Dad loved telling the story over and over again—how poor, old John couldn't find a thing on his desk for days. I loved the way he chuckled when he told stories about me. I can still hear him and see his smile. I just knew how much he loved me, and many times, I'd fall asleep at night thinking how handsome and smart he was.

~ ~ ~

By the time my parents separated, I was what mother referred to as "pleasingly plump." I wasn't the teeny-tiny, adorable, little girl anymore; and as the years of their separation and divorce went by, I began to think my dad didn't love me very much and didn't want to be around me. That must've been the reason he left us and hardly ever called or wrote or visited. He was embarrassed by me. He couldn't regale guests at parties any longer with stories of his adorable, petite daughter—because I wasn't.

I'll never forget the day Mother sat down and told us the real reason why she, Mike, and I had all moved into my sister Jo Ann's apartment. Originally, we were told that Dad was changing jobs again and would be meeting us here soon. She sat on one of the kitchen chairs, called Mike and me to come over, that she wanted to talk to us about something. She certainly didn't look happy and the first words out of her mouth were, "You're probably never going to see your dad again."

"What? Why not?" Mike and I were both stunned.

Jo Ann was there and interrupted right away. "Mother! Don't tell them that. That's not necessarily true. He just won't be living with you."

"He's been going out with other women and wants to divorce me."

She began to cry, which I realized she must've been doing a lot of lately. Her eyes were puffy, but I'd been too busy playing and just being a child to notice, or maybe I was afraid to notice.

"He even had the nerve to bring one of them around at the golf range one time when we were all there. He wanted her to *see us*." She emphasized see and us as if they were bad words.

"Oh, I think I know when you mean," I said. "That time when a lady was standing on the other side of Dad, when we were all hitting golf balls. They seemed to be talking a lot. Was that her?"

"Yes, that was her, but she was no lady!"

51

It's so weird, the things we do and don't remember. That day at the golf range had been a nice, sunny day. Mother sat on a bench and watched as Dad, Mike, and I all hit golf balls. We were in a line, each with our own tee. On the other side of Dad, the open spot was taken by a "lady" in a business looking suit with a tight skirt. She wasn't young or even pretty, but I sure remembered my dad talking with her and even introducing all of us, like we were all new friends. I can't believe he had the nerve to do such a thing. His smiling, charming face wasn't for Mother or any of us that day. It was for *her*.

Mother definitely didn't want the divorce. She was willing to forgive and forget, but Dad would have nothing to do with it. What exactly caused problems in their marriage, I'll never know for sure; but since he was seeing other women, I have a pretty good idea. I do know that hearing about their breaking up was a huge shock to Mike and me. (We never heard or saw any arguing, or unhappiness, except for those few weeks in Tulsa.) Sometimes I'd see them hug and kiss briefly when they didn't know I was there. He'd smile and walk into the living room, and it made me feel so content and happy and safe. Those feelings definitely didn't last.

Neither Mother nor Dad handled the separation and divorce the right way. They both should have made it perfectly clear to Mike and me that none of this was our fault. That they both still loved us as much as always. That although Mother had full custody of us kids, we could still see Dad, or call him, or write to him. It was impossible, though, for frequent visits because Dad lived in a different state, hundreds of miles away. He also never made many attempts to contact Mike and me. I'm not sure about Mike's feelings, but I felt like I'd been abandoned. On top of that, Mother took advantage of every spare moment to turn us against our dad, which was wrong. So, very wrong.

At least one good thing did come from this. Many years later, when I divorced my first husband, I made a promise to myself that I would not handle things the way my mother did. I kept that promise, too, even though it was difficult at times to not badmouth my ex-husband in front of my young son.

From Pigtails to Chin Hairs

Grandma and Grandpa Dorsey, 50th Wedding Anniversary 1959

Part II:

MAGICAL 1950s VACATIONS

From Pigtails to Chin Hairs

A Timeless Journey

It felt like we were flying along the highway, even though the car's tires weren't actually leaving the road. Almost all of the windows were rolled down, and my dad's left arm rested comfortably on the driver's side door, giving him that funny one-armed sunburn he got every summer. It was so hot that Dad's white, cotton, short-sleeved shirt stuck to his skin. My mother poured yet another cup of steaming hot coffee from the thermos and handed it over to him. Dad barely took his eyes off the road as he took it. I couldn't imagine why he wanted something so hot to drink. Mother brought a cold jug of Kool-Aid for my brother Mike and me.

Times like these, I wished I had a crew cut like my brother or a flattop like my dad. The force of the wind whipped my long pigtails around so much they actually stung my face every time they slapped against it.

Most of our trip consisted of two-lane highways, and sometimes Dad would have to slow down because a car or truck ahead of us was going too slow. He would turn the steering wheel to the left, so he could ease out just a little and get a look-see at what was coming. Many times, he'd have to yank the car back into our lane just in the nick of time because a car would be coming from the other direction. Mother would usually holler, "Jimmy, (that's what she called Dad) Jimmy, be careful! That was a close one!"

Other times just when he was ready to pass a car, that darn double yellow line showed up. I knew what that meant because he explained it once. No Passing!

Dad was really good at explaining things to Mike and me. He wanted us to explore and learn as much as we could and have fun while doing it. Once I leaned forward and grabbed the top of Dad's seat, so I'd be close enough for him to hear me.

"Dad, why is there water up ahead on the highway, but when we get there, it's gone? It keeps happening over and over."

"Well, that's because it's a mirage."

"A mirage? What's that?"

"It's also called an optical illusion. That means it's kind of like magic. It has to do with the hot, summer sunshine on the highway."

"Oh, okay. I think I get it." *Gosh, Dad sure was smart.*

Besides the exhilaration of driving down the highway at about a thousand miles an hour, my brother and I also had another thrill: It was the 1950s, and there were no seat belts in those days. Mike and I could flop around on the back vinyl seat and play silly games.

Another must-have item for any of our car trips, short or long, was our portable potty. It actually was nothing more than a small, old enamel bowl, always brought along in case one of us kids needed to use it. Once Dad got speeding along the highway, he didn't want to stop unless it was absolutely necessary; and he had his own rules, which were:

1) If the car needed gas.

2) If it was time to stop and eat.

We just made sure we never needed to use that potty!

One year, Dad built a wooden bench to fit in the back seat area, too. It covered the huge hump in the middle of the floor, and one of us kids would lie down and nap on it, while the other one stretched out on the vinyl seat. We also brought beach towels to throw on both of them, too— the bench in case of any loose splinters and the seat itself because it could get so hot and practically scorch our skinny, shorts-clad legs.

Even though I didn't like the long, hot ride in the car, I always looked forward to lunch at an air-conditioned, roadside restaurant. Dad was a proper gentleman and held the door open for us. How wonderful that blast of cold air felt, and it carried yummy food smells of burgers, fries, onion rings, and I didn't know what else. I also loved the shiny countertop we passed, as we walked in. It always had beautiful, homemade cakes and pies with glass tops over them—I guess to keep the flies off. Sometimes there were cherry pies with a crust that looked a bit like the pot holders Mike and I made on our looms, except the pie crusts weren't multi-colored. They were a sugary coated regular color, like the ones my mother and grandma made. Usually a slice or two would already be cut out, and the cherries and filling would ooze out a little bit. Mmmm, it made me want a slice every time.

We'd slide into a booth with shiny, red seats the same color as the round, spinning ones at the counter. They were cold and didn't stick to our bare legs, which was really comfy. I loved the paper placemats and the little glass of water that fit my hand so well, and looking at the colorful pictures on the menu. I usually knew what I wanted: a hamburger and French fries. After dad gave the waitress our order, one of my favorite reasons to stop for lunch came next—choosing songs on the little jukebox right at our booth. I couldn't believe how we could drop some dimes in the slot, flip the pages back and forth showing the song titles, choose what we wanted to hear, and listen to music—all without even leaving our seats! The four of us would eat pretty fast, though, because we were in a hurry to get to our destination: Greenfield, Iowa.

We were going to stay with Grandma and Grandpa Dorsey, mother's parents. Even though the trip seemed like it lasted about a hundred hours, summer vacation just wouldn't be the same if we didn't visit them. Nothing was better than pulling into their driveway and knowing that we were finally there! Many times, Grandma would walk down the front porch steps to greet us. She'd have on a summer dress with an apron over it, those funny looking shoes like nuns wore, and nylons rolled down to her ankles. She'd be dabbing at her face with a flowery hankie, while food aromas floated out from the kitchen window. Mmmm. I smelled fried chicken and homemade bread. It was suppertime, and grandma's cooking was even better than the food at the roadside café.

Grandma would hug Mother and Dad and ask how the trip was. She'd then lean down to give Mike and me hugs, too. Ooooh, I really didn't like being squeezed and kissed, but I knew that's what grandmas did. She had the funniest little names for Mike and me. She surely must have made them up because I'd never heard them before or since. Tinklum Toodlers. She'd always say, "Come here, you little Tinklum Toodlers!"

I'd wiggle away as fast as I could and try to run into the house, but Grandpa would sometimes be right there to stop me.

He'd have that funny, little smile on his face he always seemed to have when we were around. Dad told Mike and me it was because he thought we were the cutest grandchildren in the whole world. He was a man of few words, especially with us kids, so it was nice to know he felt that way.

He always chewed gum with a funny name: Yucatan. I'd never seen it in any of the stores at home. We usually had Juicy Fruit or Doublemint at our house. He also looked different from most men I was accustomed to being around. He was bald, which kind of scared me for some strange reason, he usually wore suspenders, and a cowboy string tie. I never saw one like that on anyone else. He also had really rough hands that he patted us on the head with when he said hello. I figured his hands might get a little softer if he'd quit using that awful, scratchy Lava soap. It was always on the bathroom sink, along with a much smoother pink bar. Grandpa's soap felt like sandpaper. I knew because I touched it once after seeing my dad wash his hands with it, too.

It's funny the things we remember. Grandpa loved to play cribbage, which I didn't understand and was too young to learn. I liked to watch, though, and thought the big piece of wood with all the tiny holes in it was neat looking. Listening to the funny way the score was added usually made me laugh, too. It was something like fifteen-two, fifteen-four, a run, and a Nob. I think!

Grandpa was a quiet spoken man, always pleasant and easy going. Grandma had an extremely peculiar voice, which I can't possibly describe. Let's just say it wasn't a soft, ladylike tone. It kind of reminded me of Ma Kettle's, especially since she bossed Grandpa around all the time. He was old and retired from his job, so he was home a lot. It got on my nerves, but I guess he'd learned to just tune her out. They'd been married for about 100 years, so he was used to it.

The furniture, pictures on the walls, and old-fashioned knick-knacks were always the same: crocheted doilies here and there, roller shades on the windows, white sheets on the beds that smelled like sunshine, and Grandma's quilt with the little, yellow sunbonnets on it. This was a place where time stood still—no matter how long between visits—and always surrounded me with feelings of love, comfort, and home.

Childhood Bliss
in Greenfield, Iowa

Our vacations in Greenfield were what dreams are made of. It's occurred to me that maybe it's for the best those yearly summer visits didn't continue as I grew older. The magic would've been gone; but oh, I'm so grateful for the memories I still carry in my heart.

In between playing outside or next door with the neighbor kids, I liked to watch my mother help Grandma with all the chores around the house. There were no dishwashers (the women were the dishwashers), no microwaves, and no "fast food" of any kind. Every dinner was a grand feast of meat, potatoes, homemade bread, and homemade pie and/or ice cream. Mike and I would take turns cranking the handle on the ice cream maker until it got too hard for us to do. Lunches the next day might be sandwiches and leftovers. I loved every aroma that came from Grandma's kitchen.

Because Mother helped Grandma so much when we were in Greenfield, her vacation was a "working" one, unlike Dad's restful getaway from his teaching position back home. That's pretty much how life was back in the 1950s though, so I don't know if Mother resented it or not. She never complained that I know of, at least I never heard her.

One of my favorite things to watch was the two of them standing around Grandma's wringer washer, doing the laundry. Back then, though, they called it doing the wash. I was particularly intrigued by that machine because we had a "modern" washer and dryer at our house. I'd never seen anything that weird-looking in my entire five or six years of life.

Well, there actually was something weirder, and it was a big problem. The washer was in the back of the basement; and to get there, I had to go around a huge, round, scary furnace. I mean *huge*. It looked like a monster with a zillion fat arms coming out of it. They were kind of curved and bent, like they were elbows. Even if I knew for sure that Grandma and Mother were in the back washer room, I'd still holler out to make sure before I got too close to IT.

"Grandma? Mother? Are you back there?" Hmm, maybe they couldn't hear me, so I tried again, yelling even louder.

"Mother? Grandma? Are you back in the wash room?"

"Yes, Becky. We're here. What do you want?" Mother hollered back.

"Oh, nothing. Just wanted to know where you were," I shouted.

At that point, I'd run around IT, leaving as much space between it and me as I possibly could.

Whew, that was another close one.

And one more big problem. The few toys that Grandma still had from when my older sisters,

Marian and Jo Ann, were little girls were also in another little room back behind the furnace. My absolute favorite was the old, two-story, metal dollhouse. It had lots of plastic furniture, some even with movable parts, like the toilet seat and the tray on the highchair! Oh, how I loved it.

Mother and Grandma would put clothes, towels, and sheets near the edge of the rollers, one at a time, and they would be grabbed and pulled right through and come out flat as pancakes on the other side. I'd been thoroughly lectured about never putting my fingers anywhere near those things, and I certainly understood why. All the water was squeezed out, and they almost looked ironed. Then everything would be carried in baskets up the stairs and outside to the back yard and pinned neatly on the clothesline. I was allowed to pin a few small things when the line sagged low enough for me to reach.

I'm sure I never watched or helped more than a few minutes of the entire process since my main purpose was to play outside, find lots of exciting things to do, and have fun. Seeing the large, white sheets stretched tight across the line and flapping lazily in the wind always gave me a feeling of happiness and security. Then off I'd run to find Mike and see what he was doing. Maybe we could go see what the neighbor kids were doing and ride bikes or play tag.

Grandma's washer wasn't the only thing that was different from what we had at our house. At home, we had things on our windows that were called venetian blinds. They were either always open or closed, never raised up high. There was nothing frightening about them. Grandma's house, on the other hand, had tons of windows, they were on all four sides of the house, and they were huge. All of them had plain, white roller shades and were very unpredictable. It seemed as if the slightest touch of the dangling drawstring would cause the shade to suddenly flutter and spin all the way up to the top, scaring the heck out of me.

It really wasn't much of a problem except at bedtime. It was so dark and quiet there—no big outdoor lights and no traffic noises. If the moon and stars were out, I'd see a glimmer of light through the shades. And the noises I heard would hopefully be just crickets. Having the windows open was okay; but if it got too windy, I'd lie in bed wondering if and when one of those shades might suddenly start flapping and rolling. Eventually I'd fall asleep, though, covered with the sweet-smelling sheets, wondering what adventures tomorrow would bring. Even a creepy furnace and intimidating window shades couldn't deter the childhood bliss I'd found in Greenfield.

Freedom of Speech

One of my first memories of the *Adair County Free Press* (in Greenfield, Iowa), which all the grownups in my family read, was the discovery that the newspaper was *not free!* Being a child of about five years old at the time, hearing the word "free" in regards to anything meant that it obviously was free, right? Not always, I was amazed to find out.

It happened one afternoon in the late 1950s when my dad let me ride "uptown" with him. At home, when we talked about going shopping, it was going "downtown." But of course, downtown was in a large city, and Greenfield's uptown was the town square. The population was about 2,000 at that time. He probably just wanted to hang around the square and talk with folks in that easy, lingering way people do in the summertime, especially in small towns. I loved seeing the farmers in their bib overalls and straw hats and the ladies in their pretty cotton dresses. It seemed like everyone knew each other, too, which always surprised and pleased me at the same time. And Dad actually did know a lot of the families there because he'd grown up in Greenfield, and many still lived there.

Whenever we visited my grandma and grandpa, I always felt transported to a faraway land because although I lived in a fairly small town myself, it was nothing like magical Greenfield. Anything you might possibly need or want could be found at any of the stores right there on the square: groceries, candy, toys, perfume, cigarettes, and even a postcard with a picture of a pig or stalks of corn right on the front of it. As we walked down the sidewalks, I'd peek into every window, and people always waved at us.

A large, two-story, red brick building stood in the center of the square. It was the courthouse and was surrounded by green grass and huge, ancient trees. I guess way back when my grandpa was the deputy sheriff of Greenfield, he must've gone in and out of that building a million times. Before that, he was one of the town's barbers and quite a handsome young man.

The weather always seemed perfect, too; it rarely rained, getting in the way of our outdoor fun. Most of the time, the sky was a shade of blue that would take your breath away with beautiful puffs of white, cotton ball clouds scattered here and there. The grass was an emerald green, and many times I'd hear a noisy lawn mower in the near distance and delight in the scent of freshly cut grass. Grandpa had what was called a push mower that didn't make much noise at all. I loved watching him use it. Sometimes, he let Mike and me try to push it, and Mike did okay; but since I was so little, it was too hard for me. I also heard something about the blades needing sharpening.

Even though I loved my own house and neighborhood, I always wished I could live there in Greenfield. I promised myself that someday when I wasn't a kid anymore, I'd move there to live forever. (That hasn't happened as of yet!)

We probably stopped somewhere that particular day and got a bottle of "pop." (Pop was another one of those words used in a strange way because where I lived, we called it "soda," not soda pop, but just soda.) Before we drove back to my grandparents' house, Dad said he wanted to pick up a *Free Press*, so we walked into the tiny newspaper's office. He knew some people there, too—members of the Sidey family who owned the newspaper (and still do as I write this). When he paid money for it, I was confused and asked him why. Why would he *pay* for a *free* newspaper?

He chuckled and explained that the "free" part was about freedom of speech, about being able to write and print whatever they wanted—not about the cost of the paper. I'm sure I didn't really understand what it meant at my young age, but my dad's explanation has stayed with me all these years.

I'm sure that neither my dad nor anyone else who knew little Becky Lewellen, would ever dream that not only would she someday become an author, but she would also write a weekly column for the esteemed *Adair County Free Press* from 2008 to 2010.

From Pigtails to Chin Hairs

Greenfield, Mayberry, and Harmony

Because of my magical summer vacations in Greenfield, I've always been drawn to small towns, whether fictional or real. One of my favorite fictional towns is Mayberry, North Carolina, home of Sheriff Andy Taylor and Deputy Barney Fife. For years and years, I was under the impression Grandpa Dorsey had been the sheriff of Greenfield when he was younger. I loved to tell the story to friends, making the comparison between dashing Harl Dorsey and the equally handsome Andy Taylor. But a few years ago, I found out Grandpa had been the *deputy*, not the sheriff. I was so surprised to learn this and also disturbed at the mental pictures of bumbling Barney. I knew, of course, my grandpa was not an inept deputy; but still, that bit of news certainly changed the daydreams that swirled around in my head.

Another favorite fictional town is Harmony, Indiana. It is the home of Pastor Sam Gardner, in the Harmony book series, written by Philip Gulley. In addition to being an author, Mr. Gulley is a pastor in the Quaker faith and lives with his wife and children in Indiana. His books are sweet, poignant, and humorous. The characters are so real you feel like you truly know them and live right in their town with them.

I stumbled across the Harmony books for the first time while browsing in a bookstore near Christmas 2003. I picked one up, flipped through the pages, read a sentence or two, and knowing right then that I'd like it, I bought it. After reading two more books in the series, I decided to write to Mr. Gulley and tell him how much I enjoyed his books. I naively included a couple of my newspaper columns from that time, asking for his critique and advice. Naturally, I hoped for a response, but never really expected one.

Much to my surprise and pleasure, Mr. Gulley replied with a handwritten note. He thanked me for my letter and columns, and said he enjoyed my writing and to keep it up. I was thrilled, to say the least. Receiving his letter of encouragement gave me such a lift. I felt that not only was it okay for me to keep writing, but maybe I had some talent, too.

I had the privilege to meet him when he was one of the speakers at the Missouri Writers Guild Conference in St. Charles, Missouri, in 2007. We've kept in touch when I had some exciting publishing news, and he always took the time to reply, sending his sincere best wishes. And when the time came that I was actually almost finished with this memoir, I asked if he could possibly read a few chapters and write a book blurb for me, which he did without hesitation. What a kind and gracious man. I can't possibly say enough wonderful things about Mr. Philip Gulley, or thank him enough.

Greenfield, Mayberry, and Harmony: three wonderfully unique and special towns. Whether you arrive at them in person, by watching television, or by reading a book, you're sure to be in small-town-heaven. Maybe I'll see you there.

From Pigtails to Chin Hairs

Piggy Back Toes & Coffee Can Spittoons

Recently, I told my husband, Ron, that he and I are turning into my Aunt Grace and Uncle Albert. I've described them to him quite a few times over the past 30 years; but since he usually forgets (or ignores) most of my ramblings, I once again related my memories to him.

Actually, they were my great aunt and great uncle; but to my brother and me, they were always just plain old Aunt Grace and Uncle Albert.

My brother, Mike, and I loved everything about our Greenfield vacations. I liked to visit Aunt Grace, and Mike enjoyed being with Uncle Albert. Even as very young kids, we were allowed to walk the few blocks from our grandparents' house over to theirs. Ah, those were the days.

I adored Aunt Grace. She was short and pudgy, with her white hair pinned up into a bun. Usually a few unruly tresses hung down along her ears and soft pink cheekbones, and she'd have a few beads of sweat on her forehead. I knew that was because she worked so hard.

"Well, what are you kids up to today?" she'd ask, as she shuffled back and forth in the tiny kitchen in her tattered canvas shoes. The entire toe section was cut out, so her little, crooked toes wouldn't be so squished. She didn't have just hammertoes. She had a couple of toes that actually rode piggy back on top of each other! I remember thinking how both funny and sad that was, and secretly wished I would never have such an infliction when *I* got *old*. (Unfortunately, that was one of many wishes that did not come true.)

As I watched her go about her work, I would reply, "Dad is going to drive us to Piper's this afternoon! I have seventy-five cents to spend on whatever I want!" (Piper's was the town's dime store.)

Grace was always sweet and happy, and it was common for wonderful aromas to waft from her oven, most likely that of homemade bread or sugar cookies. And of course, she always gave Mike and me sample bites or entire portions of her scrumptious baked goods. I spent most of my time in the kitchen with her, while Mike was in another room with Albert.

Uncle Albert was totally the opposite. In comparison to Aunt Grace's soft, smooth skin and plump body, he was thin, with a bony, scratchy face. He always sat in his rocking chair in the sparse living room. It contained a small couch, a black & white TV, an end table, and a game of checkers. He was surrounded by newspapers, which Aunt Grace laid all over the floor. There were also a few large, empty coffee cans placed in strategic areas, just for his use. I couldn't imagine why all that was there and had never seen such a strange and messy room before.

Uncle Albert constantly had a cigar in his mouth, and the papers and cans were for tobacco juice "spits and spills." *Ooh, yucky*. That alone scared me somewhat, but I was really frightened by his rough, dry hands. They shook when he wanted me to come closer, so he could give me a nickel or a dime to spend at the store. I always thought he had "bug eyes," too. To top it all off, he also had horrible toes, but they weren't crooked like Grace's. No, he was always barefooted, and his toenails were huge, thick, and yellow!

Grace hollered from the kitchen sometimes, "Albert! You be careful with that cigar, especially around those kids! And don't make a mess!" He would just shake his head and act like he didn't hear her. Then he'd spit into one of the cans and continue to chew on his soggy cigar.

Mike wasn't a bit afraid of him and really liked being around him. He seemed to think Uncle Albert was hilarious. I guess he understood his speech better than I did because I had no idea what he said most of the time. All I could do was stare at those bulging eyes, look at his hands shake, and try not to look at his feet. I was glad to have a big brother who stayed by my side and took care of me, even though he was only seven and a-half years old, and I was a mere six.

Our parents told us that Uncle Albert loved kids, especially Mike and me, and how much he and Grace both enjoyed our visits. They were only able to have one child and had no grandchildren of their own. That's too bad because they were wonderful people.

These days, my husband Ron not only smokes cigars and has rough, dry hands, but he also seems to have selective hearing. I, on the other hand, am getting quite plump, have soft skin, touches of gray in my hair, and crooked toes. It's only a matter of time before newspapers and tin cans appear on the floor, and my shoes need holes in the toe area.

Becky in St. Philip's school uniform, 8th Grade, 1966-67

Part III:

THE BITTERSWEET YEARS

From Pigtails to Chin Hairs

He Called Me "The Tank"

When I was 12 years old, my brother Mike called me "The Tank." The reason being I was short and fat, kind of square and heavy like an army tank. He also instructed our two preschool-age nieces, Tammy and Renee, to call me "Big Fat Aunt Becky." When they did, he howled like a laughing hyena.

That summer, I would curl up in a chair in our living room and cry, for no particular reason, other than the fact that I was miserable. Remember those "hoop chairs"? They were shallow and circular, with narrow, wooden legs. Ours was padded vinyl, turquoise, and really wasn't a bit comfortable except when someone sat in a curled, fetal position, which I did rather well. (See a small part of it in the photo of me? Maybe I don't look particularly fat there, but I was 40 lbs. overweight, and in the 1960s *that* was fat. There wasn't a multitude of obese kids in those days and classrooms usually only had one "fat kid.")

One particular Saturday afternoon, I watched *The Member of the Wedding* on TV and cried through the entire film. I related to Frankie's loneliness. I certainly wasn't part of the "in crowd" and going through adolescence is hard enough on a girl, but add to that being short, overweight, and pimply, and dealing with the heartbreak of psoriasis and athlete's foot. (I found out my already ugly hammer toes were allergic to the rubber in flip-flops and canvas sneakers like Aunt Grace always wore.) To top it all off, my extremely limp, lifeless hair contained dandruff. I felt so unlovable and couldn't imagine anything ever good happening to me. I was a MESS.

As I got older my looks improved somewhat, but my teenage years didn't consist of an ugly duckling turning into a beautiful swan. No, that certainly didn't happen.

It sure didn't help that The New Thing in fashion was Twiggy—and go-go boots and empire waist dresses and clingy fabrics—everything I wanted to wear, but looked ridiculous in because of my weight. Mother did relent after I begged and begged for some white go-go boots. All the girls dancing on the TV show, Hullabaloo, wore them and they were so cute. The popular girls at school had them, too. Surely, I could be popular and cute, too, right? Uh…no. It also didn't take long to realize they hurt my feet and really weren't worth the price. They stayed on the floor of my bedroom closet for years, all scuffed and unappreciated, just like I deemed I was.

It's So Nice to Have a Man Around the House

My mother unconsciously taught me that a woman's life without a husband was difficult, lonely, and downright scary.

When I was thirteen, a door-to-door salesman knocked on our front door one evening; and when she opened the door, he asked to see the man of the house. Without really thinking, she said that she was divorced and had no husband. I don't even remember what he was selling; but the minute he left, she was so upset and worried that since he knew there wasn't a man in our house, he might come back to "get us." The thought of that happening scared me too, but after a while having Mike and Jo Ann also at home made me feel better. The three of us had to continue reassuring Mother that everything was okay and to quit worrying.

Being a divorced Catholic in the early 1960s was almost unheard of. In fact, divorce in general was fairly rare, and certainly nothing like today. In this twenty-first century, a kid who has a stepfamily is almost the norm.

Because of the scarcity of other divorced women for Mother to associate with and also her lack of self-esteem, she didn't have many friends. She referred to herself as "the fifth wheel" and wallowed in self-pity. She talked about our "broken home" as if it was the worst possible thing in the entire world. The actual word "divorce" insinuated something horrible, like a disease and needed to be whispered. I can still hear Tammy Wynette singing about "D-i-v-o-r-c-e."

And although I honestly did feel sorry for Mother, Mike, and myself, I kept trying to be a "normal" kid, having fun and enjoying my young life. But it was a difficult situation to deal with most of the time.

Lost on a Continental Trailways Bus

When Dad was married to his second wife, Twila, they lived in Columbus, Ohio, for a few years. He must've invited me to come and visit the summer I was 13 years old because I don't think I would've done the asking. We didn't talk on the phone; we barely wrote letters; and I hated his wife, so why would I want to stay with them for a week? I'd never met Twila, so the only reason for my hatred was because my father was married to **her** instead of my mother.

Somehow, Mother and/or Jo Ann persuaded me to go see Dad, so I relented. It surprised me because I'd been "taught" for so many years to despise him. He sent the money, though, for a round-trip bus ticket for one. For the first time in my life, I'd be traveling completely by myself, which wasn't all that unusual in those days.

The trip was about 400 miles with several stops along the way for boarding, deboarding, and rest stops. I remember nothing of that ride, only the fact I arrived safe and sound at my destination.

Dad met me at the bus stop, hugged me, and took my suitcase. He tried to make small talk while we walked to his car, a pale blue Ford of some kind.

"How was the ride? Did you have any problems during your trip?"

"It was fine. Just kind of long and boring, but I had some snacks and read my book," I replied.

The only thing I remember about my visit was going shopping one afternoon with Twila. As she drove the two of us to an upscale department store, she tried to make small talk, just as Dad had done when he picked me up at the bus station. God, I was visiting two complete strangers. After she parked the car, we went inside and found the girls section, and she said she'd buy me a shirt or slacks.

It seemed like we walked up and down the clothes aisles forever. I really didn't like any of the items she pulled off the rack to suggest, and I didn't really see much I liked—anywhere. Finally, I decided on a cotton shirt with three-quarter length, ruffled sleeves in a large, loud plaid of blues and reds. Even after trying it on in the dressing room and seeing my fat, little self in the mirror, I still insisted on getting it. I liked it.

And what did Twila have to say about it? She said something to the effect of: "Becky, you really shouldn't wear something like that with the large pattern. You should look for something that makes you look slimmer."

Nice. This coming from a woman I'd never met before and already hated. My visit couldn't end fast enough.

On my trip back home to St. Louis, the bus stopped at a diner that included a gift shop. I became a bit too engrossed in gazing at all the pretty boxes of note cards and stationery, teen magazines, and candy. Much later, I was told the bus departure was announced over the loud speaker three times, but it certainly fell on deaf ears.

By the time I realized my bus had gone and left me, I became a bit hysterical. Someone "in charge" talked to me and got me a seat on the next bus headed my way which was quite a while later.

Finally, the bus pulled into the Downtown St. Louis Trailways Bus Terminal. After getting off the bus, the passengers, including myself, waited to get their suitcases from the underneath compartment. I can still remember the smells and sounds of the outside area of that old bus station: blasts of exhaust pipes and gassy fumes; cigar and cigarette smoke mixed with stale perfume and body odor.

When I walked inside, I immediately saw Mother and Jo Ann sitting in the waiting area. They jumped up and the three of us hugged as if we'd never let go of each other. They told me how worried they were when I didn't get off the correct bus and Jo Ann then asked the bus station supervisor to call and find out what happened to me! That's how they knew I'd be on the later bus.

Even though I wished I had my dad in my life, I realized after seeing him that he was no longer the dad I remembered. He wouldn't be the right "fit" for our family anymore, but that still didn't stop me from dreaming and fantasizing about having our old, perfect family back together again.

Memories of Mike

I'd have to say that when I was a little girl, my brother Mike and I had a typical sibling relationship. He was only fifteen months older than me and we were great playmates. Together we watched *The Three Stooges* and *Wrestling at the Chase* on TV, which led us to our own crazy antics. Mother would holler when she'd see or hear us wrestling around on the floor.

"Mike and Becky! Quit that right this minute. One of you is going to get hurt!"

"Aww…no we won't. We're just playing and having fun."

The next thing you knew, one of us, and 99% of the time it was I, would be crying because of *accidentally* being punched, slapped, or thrown onto the floor. I know I was only five or six years old during that time.

Knowing my fear of the dark, during those same years, one of Mike's favorite things to do was to scare the living daylights out of me. When it would be nighttime, he'd say, "Let's go play in our room!" To which I always happily agreed. (Ah, I was so trusting and naïve.) We'd scamper into the room and begin to play a game when all of a sudden he'd let out a bloodcurdling scream, turning the light switch off as he ran out the door, slamming it shut behind him. I'd run out seconds later, as soon as I could find the doorknob, squealing and crying hysterically. He'd be standing nearby laughing his head off. I think he got into trouble the first couple of times, but I fell for it so often that it just became Dad saying, "Mike, don't scare your sister in the dark."

A few years later, after our parents were divorced, Mike could make everyone laugh without even trying. Funny things would just "happen" to him, and he would make the most of the situations. I remember a few distinct occasions that happened over the course of one or two winters that still make me smile when I think of them. One is that while walking to church on a cold Sunday morning, his Hush Puppies somehow got stuck to the icy sidewalk, and he couldn't move! Knowing his usual antics, my mother kept telling him to quit goofing around until she realized that he literally was stuck to the ice. Mike took full advantage of the situation and provided his usual clowning around. Jo Ann and I laughed hysterically, while Mother tried to figure out what to do.

Finally Mother went inside, got a pan of hot water, and poured a little of it on the sidewalk to loosen his shoes. That did the trick, and I'm pretty sure he walked the rest of the way in the grassy areas.

Another extremely cold Sunday, Jo Ann, Mike, and I were at Mass, completely bundled up in our heavy winter coats. This walking all the time was getting old, but we didn't have a car and couldn't afford one, either. As we knelt at the Communion Rail, all of a sudden one of the shiny buttons on Mike's coat popped off and went soaring up towards the altar. I guess he had on one too many layers that day, and the thread decided to call it quits. Of course, being in a situation where we shouldn't laugh, it made us want to giggle all the more. Why something as silly as a button flying through the air was funny, I couldn't say. It just was. We couldn't help but do that silent, shoulder-shaking laugh and a bit of snorting, too. Luckily, the button didn't hit the priest or the altar boy, but it pinged a couple of times as it bounced around the marble floor and steps. I could feel many pairs of eyes scanning the front of church, wondering who the culprits were. The three of us managed to get through the rest of Mass without causing any more commotion, but I don't think we could've said what the closing hymn was. We were too busy trying to keep solemn faces and weren't doing a very good job of it.

A year or two after the button episode, my brother decided he wanted to be in charge of picking out our Christmas tree. He was probably about14 years old at the time, and I guess he felt like the man of the house. Just he and Jo Ann went to the tree lot that year. Well, in his desire to have a really huge tree, he brought one home that was probably four feet taller than our ceiling. In order to make it fit, he had to saw it off, but he didn't do it at the trunk. He cut the four feet right off the top. Why? I don't know. But we had a very tall, very flat-topped tree that year. Somehow, he had the idea years before Clark Griswold did in *Christmas Vacation*.

Faith, hope, and a sense of humor have always been important in my life, and I've learned you don't have to have a perfect childhood or a perfect life to be truly happy. The joy just comes from within, from your daily appreciation of life, and from whatever warm memories you hold in your heart.

Schmock! Schmock!

Gary was a grade school classmate of mine—the class clown. He was tall, lanky, and toothpick thin, a bit like a male Olive Oyl. Even his leather belt pulled to the tightest notch couldn't keep his white uniform shirt tucked in. He must've been really uncomfortable every minute of the day. Those sixth grade desks weren't constructed for his kind of build. Slouched in his seat and knees scrunched up, his size 11 penny loafers hit the desk in front of him. Gangly arms flailed as he grabbed for pens, paper, and books—all stored in the underneath compartment. Bending over sideways and trying to find the appropriate item was nearly impossible, as was twisting on the seat, leaning way over, and looking between your legs, only to see everything upside down. In poor Gary's case, his head would sometimes thump on the tile floor.

He sat in the last desk, in the last row, next to the wall of windows. I'm sure he spent a lot of time gazing outside, probably daydreaming, or looking for something interesting to occupy his mind, since school was so boring. With no air conditioning, the windows were often cranked open, allowing whatever breeze existed to drift inside.

Classrooms containing 50 students (five rows with ten desks each) were standard there: St. Philip's Grade School in East St. Louis, Illinois. The teachers, mostly nuns, always had the upper hand; and for the most part, everyone behaved. Nobody wanted their knuckles smacked with the wooden ruler or to be sent to the principal's office, receiving a threat to call our parents. Some of those nuns could bring many kids to tears just by yelling.

I usually received good grades in arithmetic—a-rat-in-the-house-might-eat-the-ice-cream. (I wonder how many kids learned that saying? Those little spelling tricks are still with me, as are zillions of song lyrics; yet, I can't remember where I put something or why I walked into a certain room.) When it came to word problems, though, my eyes would glaze over, my brain snap shut, and I felt as if I were reading a foreign language: If two trains are traveling the same distance, but at different speeds, how long will it take . . . blah, blah, blah? *Please don't yell at me, Sister Josameana. I honestly don't get it. Just give me an F.*

Boys like Gary sometimes made school fun and other times just plain tolerable. Besides his usual antics of mumbling and joking around with guys nearby, every now and then for no particular reason, he'd let out a riotous, high-pitched screech of "Schmock! Schmock!"

The first time it happened, Sister Josameana almost jumped out of her chair, visibly startled with frown lines forming on her forehead. She'd been looking down, flipping through the day's history lesson.

"Who did that?" she shrieked with pursed lips.

No replies, just some chortles and knee slaps from the boys and a few giggles from the girls. I almost swallowed the Luden's Cherry cough drop I'd just popped into my mouth. Sister stood up and placed her palms flat on her desk, scanning the room with her steely eyes.

"I said who did that?"

Then, complete quiet settled around the classroom. No one was about to point toward Gary, not even us girls. We had to stick together in things like this. Class clowns kept us sane during those awkward middle school years, especially when we had crabby teachers.

Sister Josameana was definitely not one of the fun nuns. I think she hated teaching. She never smiled. She didn't like to joke around. She should've retired and been living at the Ancient Retired Nun's Home. She was just wrinkly, old, and mean.

I loved Gary's shrieks of "Schmock! Schmock!" because they were so unexpected and so hilarious, and also because I felt part of a special group knowing where he'd heard it: *The Steve Allen Show.* (I was pretty sure most of the kids in my class weren't hip enough to know about it or watch it, especially the other girls.)

Many nights, I'd stay up late and watch TV with Mike and Jo Ann. Steve Allen was genuinely, spontaneously funny—many times cackling at his own blunders. He'd start giggling when things didn't go as expected and slide down his chair, making goofy faces and roaring hysterically. The more he laughed, the more contagious it became. And then there it was, "Schmock! Schmock!"

I loved the times the three of us spent together. I'm convinced that's when my kooky sense of humor began to develop and take root. Thank goodness—because I consider it one of my best assets and it has seen me through everything life has thrown at me.

Sleep was never difficult on those nights we watched Steve Allen. It would be late, I'd laughed a lot, and I'd be really tired. Right before I conked out, though, I wondered what the next day would bring. Would class be monotonous, half-way interesting, or loads of fun? Who could possibly know? *Schmock! Schmock!*

Boyfriends Schmoyfriends

Have I mentioned I didn't keep a diary? There wasn't any need for one. I had crushes on various boys, all unrequited loves. I day-dreamed off and on about one particular guy from the day I met him, when I was 10 years old, until years later when I ran off and eloped, and no, it wasn't with him.

I grew up wanting true love, a romantic wedding, and a perfect marriage, living Happily Ever After. I'm quite sure my parents' divorce had a lot to do with those wistful dreams. As I matured though, I knew nobody could live up to those longings and yet . . .

Just a glimpse of him walking down the school hallway toward me. We passed each other, and it appeared he smiled at me. Really? I looked around. I didn't see any other girls looking at him, so he must've been smiling at me. *Sigh.* In the cafeteria, the day he was the official lunch-ticket-taker, he smiled, too. *Sigh.* But, he smiled at everybody.

During the girls' softball games, sometimes he was the umpire the day I pitched. The umps didn't stand behind the batter and catcher like they did in baseball. No, they stood a few feet behind the pitcher and just slightly to the side, providing a good view of home plate. (At least that was the intention.) We were so close in distance, yet so far away in our feelings, never to be more than friends.

I actually did have one boyfriend in grade school; and during the time we "went together," I never thought about that other guy. I think we were in the seventh grade, (I wasn't in my totally disgusting stage at that time) and I remember it as a sweet romance, although I don't know how it began exactly. Maybe he walked me home from school, and as we talked, it just kind of happened. He called me almost every night, and as in most homes in the 1960s, we just had one phone.

Ours hung on the kitchen wall. It wasn't one of the cool, pastel colors. No, we couldn't afford those; so ours was the plain old black kind. It was during this time that I also wished with all my heart that I had a pink princess phone. In the big scheme of things, though, that wasn't at the top of my wish list.

All we ever did was hold hands and I only remember one kiss....on the cheek. Like I said, it was sweet. It was also short lived, and it's strange that I don't remember how we became a "couple" nor do I remember how or why he broke up with me. I think it was over the phone, and I'm not sure he gave a reason. It may have had something to do with the fact that I had neither a Twiggy, nor a Raquel Welch body. In the next day or two, he already had a new girlfriend. After that, it was safer to stick with my secret crushes, and there were many of them.

Looking back at my grade school and high school years, I realize that I pretty much developed a crush on almost any guy who actually spoke kindly to me, or joked around with me. In other words, any male figure that paid some attention to me. (Hmm, can you say "Daddy Issues?") I even thought I was serious about a guy or two, but realized I didn't know what real love felt like. That explains so much, and especially why I married my first husband, John.

From Pigtails to Chin Hairs

How Could She Do That to Me?

Speaking of crushes, when I was 16 years old, I had a huge, secret crush on a cousin of mine, a first cousin no less. It was a secret that was all mine – until a conversation overheard by my mother one summer night crushed it. She completely overreacted and went berserk, humiliating the hell out of me.

It all began in 1968 or '69. Mother and I were visiting my grandma and other relatives in Iowa. My cousin, Alex, stopped in at Grandma's to visit before he went to his next military assignment: Vietnam.

I think that was the first time I met him in person. Sure, I knew about him but our paths had never crossed. He was a bit older than I was, maybe by five years? He was handsome, nice, and actually talked to me, which I found very appealing. I don't remember any particular discussion, but I must've given him my address and said I'd write to him. (I loved to write and receive letters and had lots of pen pals over the years. I also thought it would be nice for him to get something at mail call, even if it was only from a younger relative.)

And so our correspondence began.

Never once did he insinuate *anything* romantic or lead me on in *any* way. God, no! Never. Ever. Ever. In my teenage heart though, my one-sided crush deepened as the months went by. It was similar to infatuations girls have for movie stars, I guess. I knew nothing would ever happen, but I couldn't help myself from thinking, could I?

We wrote back and forth for quite a few months, maybe his entire tour. When it was over and he came back to the States, he came to St. Louis to visit my mother and me. That was probably in 1970. I was so happy and excited to see him, mostly because I had worried every single day that he might become another casualty of the war.

Sometime later in that summer, my mother and I drove up to his parents' place. They lived in either Iowa or one of the Dakotas at that time. It seems like there were several relatives there, plus Alex's girlfriend Mary, and we all stayed in little cabins of some sort. Some of the details of that visit are rather hazy, maybe because of our quick exit, but the outcome is deeply etched into my mind.

The cabins had twin beds, and my mother and I shared one. The second night we were there, Mary came by and stayed for a while. She was so nice, and I really needed to talk to someone about my feelings for Alex. And heck, why not his girlfriend? She knew what a great guy he was.

When I thought Mother was asleep, I poured my heart out to her as quietly as I could. I cried and she listened the entire time, offered some comforting words, and promised she'd never breathe a word of it. Even though I knew I shouldn't feel the way I did about a first cousin, I couldn't help it. And besides, they were only feelings, nothing else.

Well, my mother overheard us talking and *totally* overreacted. The minute Mary left the cabin, she sat up in her bed and began to hiss at me.

"I heard you talking, Becky. He is your *first* cousin, and that is *a sin!* Don't you know that? What's the matter with you?! And what have you been doing?"

"God, Mother! I haven't done anything. How could you lie there and listen to us? It's none of your business! And besides, if you'd heard everything I said, you'd know there was nothing to it."

I don't remember what else was said by either of us, except for her saying we were leaving first thing in the morning.

"But why? We haven't stayed as long as we planned. I don't want to leave yet."

"Well, we're going home tomorrow. I'm too upset to stay, and that's that," she said.

She was upset? *She* was embarrassed?

When we walked out to her crappy, blue Nova the next day, I couldn't look at anyone. I wasn't able to say goodbye and kept staring at the ground. She gave some lame excuse about leaving, and I have no idea what the others thought. As I climbed into the car, I managed to glance back at Mary and Alex. She looked sympathetic, and he looked clueless. Good. I didn't want him to know. It would've made my humiliation worse, if that was even possible.

Mother got into the driver's seat, started the engine, and drove off. I slumped in the back seat, crying most of the 500 miles home. She spoke a few words, but I had nothing to say to her. It was only a little over a year later that I left home.

That Crowbar Changed Everything

My mother told me in so many words she thought I was nuts. She honestly believed my accident at Woolworth's—involving an ice machine, a crowbar, and my head—caused severe brain damage. In her way of thinking, it was the only possible explanation for what she considered the erratic behavior I developed soon after.

It was the summer of 1971, and I'd just graduated from Lindbergh High School. Carole King's album *Tapestry* was number one on the charts and remained there for weeks. I played that LP so many times on my cheapie, plastic stereo the grooves almost wore out. Not only did I memorize every word to every song, but I could belt them out with the best of them, whether sitting at my old, wooden desk, dancing around my room, or flopped on top of my pink, floral bedspread. Who could ever forget "(You Make Me Feel Like) A Natural Woman" or "I Feel the Earth Move" and of course, "You've Got a Friend."

My high school graduation class consisted of 1,000 students, totally engulfing me as one of the many unseen, unknown girls. I was lost in a sea of gold and green graduation caps and gowns on a sweltering June evening.

Oh how I wished my mother and I had never moved. I'd been happy at St. Teresa's Academy, the all-girl Catholic high school with its small enrollment and lots of friendships. What a culture shock— going from there to a huge, co-ed public high school, especially in the middle of my junior year. I felt lost and lonely even with the few friends I had. And I had no one to blame but myself. I'm the one who urged and pushed Mother about moving out of the house we rented. Jo Ann and Mike had both moved away, and it was just the two of us. We had peeping Tom problems and felt afraid to live in East St. Louis any longer. I assumed I'd be welcomed as the new girl, and everything would be fine. Plus, my friend Barb and her family had moved to the same area, where we wanted to live, and I was sure I'd see her in some of my classes and at lunch. Wrong! I never saw her at school, and I wasn't welcomed at all—not by kids or teachers. In such a large school, I guess nobody knew if you were just transferring classes or completely new to the school. Whatever it was, nobody cared.

At times, I had considered myself kind of cute, maybe like a work in progress. I wore my hair long and straight as was the style, but it was baby fine and a color I referred to as dirty dishwater brown. I also wore glasses and couldn't afford any of the cool clothes and accessories the rich girls wore, and there were plenty of them in that school district. I was shy and didn't have much of a figure. I thought I had a pretty good personality, but who cares at that age?

You know the old line, about when a guy tries to set up his buddy on a blind date:

"Well, is she pretty?"

"She's nice. She's really nice."

"Yeah, but is she *pretty*?"

I did have a few dates but never with The One. I wasn't sure what real love should feel like, although I knew about the chemistry between two people and all that. I'd seen it in the movies and on TV. I just didn't experience any fireworks in high school. At times, I felt the warmth of tiny embers lingering since the year puberty walloped me with my first secret love and the next and the next. Ah, unrequited love.

All through grade school and the first two years of high school, I was sure I'd go to college. I always made good grades without really trying. Thinking back, I'm sure straight A's might have been possible, except in any kind of math course. Perhaps a scholarship, too, had I put a little more effort into it.

Mother didn't have money for college, and maybe grants and loans weren't as accessible then. I don't remember hearing anything about attempts to find any help. All I know is, I wasn't able to go and I was terribly disappointed. My parents had been divorced for ten years; and although Dad assured us he'd pay tuition for both my brother and me, it never happened. There was also the promise of a used car after I got out of high school. That didn't magically appear, either.

Something occurred during the fall of my junior year that shattered all my hopes about college. My brother Mike graduated in 1969, and was thrilled to be accepted by the university of his dreams. Early in his first semester, though, he received notice that his tuition hadn't been paid and was given financial papers for our dad to fill out.

But Dad refused, saying, "It's none of their damn business how much money I make."

So, no paperwork filled out. No financial help. No payments made. Mike's goals were destroyed by his own father. How in the world could he do such a thing? The most unbelievable part of the whole scenario was that Dad made plenty of money, although the divorce settlement didn't appear that way.

(Mother always complained about "robbing Peter to pay Paul," and I got so tired of hearing that.) I'll never forget the day Mike had to move out of his dorm room. Mother and I were there to help, but all I remember is watching him and his roommate carry boxes out to her old Chevy Nova. Mike was so miserable; I felt sorry for him, and I also knew right then and there that my college dreams went up in smoke along with his.

Mike and I were never the kind of brother and sister who confided in each other. In fact, he seemed to just tolerate me as we got older. So we never talked about his disappointment or hurt or anger. He changed a lot after that, but I didn't see him much.

Most of my friends moved away in the fall of '71. Their parents drove them across the state or across the country to begin the next step in their lives—going to college and living away from home. When I was younger, I thought I wanted to teach; but I wasn't sure about that either. I assumed once I was in college things would just fall into place, and I'd know what I wanted to do with my life. So much for assumptions.

Realizing I needed to learn some job skills, I took typing and shorthand in my senior year of high school. I found them both challenging and fun, like learning a new language. I loved becoming skilled in typing without looking at the keys—and on an electric typewriter, no less! At home, we had an ancient, black, manual one in a carrying case. That thing weighed a ton and was worse than carrying around a bowling ball. (It did come in handy a couple of years later, but not for any reasons one might think.)

Fun and easy, shorthand class fascinated me for several reasons. Our instructor Ms. Carlson made the decision to teach after years of being a legal secretary. She kept us captivated with tales of lavish law firms and handsome lawyers. I loved her style and her jewelry—jingly bracelets with earrings and necklaces to match and brightly colored scarves tied around her neck or up around a ponytail. Beautiful clothes that surely weren't bargain basement outfits. Everything coordinated perfectly with just the right amount of perfume. I knew then I wanted to become a well-paid secretary to a highly successful businessman. I yearned for the monetary things I'd grown up without. It was time for ME. I had to choose my own path in life. I.Was.Ready. Mother already had the idea that I was going to get a job, share the apartment with her, and help pay the bills just like Jo Ann had done. That was definitely not in my plan. I just had to get away.

As I scanned the want ads, I kept seeing ones with the employment agency of Snelling and Snelling. I'd heard of them and decided they should be able to find a great paying job for me. Contacting their office, though, proved to be a big waste of my time. I knew agents made commissions on the jobs they filled, but I had no idea the length they would go. My agent sent me on positions I'm sure she knew I wasn't qualified for. How could she not after the paperwork I filled out? I would drive for miles and miles, just to find out after arriving for my interview that they needed an experienced secretary. Driving there and back in a car with no air conditioning in the hot, humid St. Louis summer, I became dejected and angry. It didn't take long to discover I couldn't get hired without any job experience, and I couldn't get any job experience because no one would hire me!

Okay, Plan B: get whatever job I could in order to earn some money—maybe enough to get my own apartment. I accepted a waitressing job at a local F. W. Woolworth's, which included a lunch counter, tables, and booths. I was given a white uniform (Oooh, I felt like a nurse!) and one of the huge menus, which I was told to memorize overnight. *(Are you kidding me?)* And I had to report to work the next day.

No matter what time my shift began, the various aromas floating through the luncheonette made my mouth water: hamburgers, French fries, onions, patty melts, hot dogs, and all those other hundreds of items on the menu. Mmmm. The usual order was a hamburger, fries, and a coke. Besides the wonderful smells, I really enjoyed hearing all the typical diner noise: the clink of glasses and silverware, sodas and malts being slurped through straws, the din of voices, a child's squeal or laugh.

During my break, I roamed the aisles and checked out the sales. The retailer was called various names by its shoppers: Woolworth's, Woolies, the Five & Dime, the Dime Store. Think of it as a miniature Walmart or K-Mart. It sold all kinds of things: sheets, towels, socks, perfume, shaving lotion—you name it. And oh, the candy counter! What lovely whiffs floated through the store from that little gem. Small paper bags filled with customers' choices of freshly-made candies, sold by the pound and weighed on shiny, hanging scales. What a great place to work—at least for some people and in some of the departments.

It didn't take long to discover I wasn't cut out to be a waitress. I was cheerful with the customers and usually managed to turn in their orders correctly, but I was terrible when it came to money transactions. There weren't computerized checkout systems in the early 1970s, and our cash register was an outdated monstrosity even for those days. A huge, bronze antique in my opinion—it must've been left over from the 1890s. It sat on top of our back work counter and seemed to loom above and over me. I was five feet tall with shoes on and weighed 100 pounds. It required all the strength I could muster up just to push the old-fashioned buttons. As I did, little numbers would flip up in the glass window: 59¢, 99¢, $1.25, and so on. It added up the total, but it certainly didn't show what change was due.

I would panic, trying to calculate the correct figures in my number-challenged brain. The longer it took me to stand with my back to the customer—mentally trying to do subtraction with my fingers and toes as I pulled bills and coins from the drawer—the more I agonized. I have no idea how many times I gave back the wrong amount, but one instance has always stayed with me.

I watched a gentleman walk away counting his money. He then turned and walked back toward me. I held my breath hoping he wasn't going to be mad and yell, saying I shortchanged him. I let out a sigh of relief, as he handed me a wad of bills and coins, mumbling something about getting too much money back. To this day, whenever I hear someone say, "Here, I have a nickel. Will that help?" I swear I break out into a cold sweat!

When I'd only worked there for a couple of weeks, the evening arrived that would prove to be my last one there. Our soda fountain had Coca Cola, 7-Up, Orange Crush, and root beer. No diet sodas in those days. (They weren't readily available until a few years later, and the first one I tried was Tab with its god-awful taste.) Anyway, next to that was our stainless steel, six-foot-high, ice-making machine. We would slide open the waist-high door, slightly lean in, scoop the plastic glasses through the crushed ice, and then fill them up with the beverages. Often the ice stuck together in gigantic chunks and needed some heavy-duty chopping.

One evening during closing, there were just two of us working. The veteran waitress was in the back putting food away and told me to chop up the ice. (When thinking back on it, I can't imagine why the ice needed chopping at night. Wouldn't it just need to be chopped again in the morning after a long night's clump?) For reasons still unknown and obviously not apparent to the health department at that time, an old crowbar was used for the task. It was kept on top of the massive contraption. Since I was so short, I had to stand on my tiptoes in order to reach it. I managed to grab hold of it, pull it down, and chop, chop, chop the ice. When I finished, I again stood on my tiptoes and pushed it back to where it had been, or so I thought. I turned and before I could walk away, I felt a strange *sting* on the top of my head and heard a *clang-clunk* on the linoleum floor. As if in slow motion, I turned and looked down and saw the crowbar and then looked back to the top of the ice machine. I touched the top of my head, as I was trying to figure out exactly what happened. When I brought my hand down and looked at it, I saw blood on my fingers and instantly dropped to the floor in a dead faint.

A few months later, I eloped with my first husband, a guy I'd known for only thirty days.

~ ~ ~

Mother: "You know, Becky, you haven't been the same since that crowbar fell on your head."

From Pigtails to Chin Hairs

Becky in Ft. Bliss house, a few days after Scott was born 1972.

(Notice the decorative lawn chair in the living room, and the towel curtains!)

Part IV:

THE GOOD, THE BAD, & THE DEPARTURE

From Pigtails to Chin Hairs

Excuse Me, Would You Mind Taking a Survey?

Shortly after John and I eloped, I became pregnant, which certainly wasn't a surprise to any of my friends or family. Everyone thought I must've been pregnant before we got married. Why else would a seemingly sensible eighteen-year-old girl elope with a guy she knew for *one* month? Well, it was a shock to John and me, too. I can tell you that.

He was a car mechanic and had no health insurance coverage. I had no job. After the Woolworth's incident, I just kind of drifted along, wasting my days and nights, hanging out with other unemployed high school graduates, which made me depressed. I decided I wanted to be just a housewife and mother, but I never intended it to happen so fast. Looking back, I find it both funny and remarkable that John's military career was the result of an unexpected pregnancy.

He signed up because a buddy of his said the Army provided free health care to military men and their families. Just like that. We didn't want my health care or that of our baby's to depend on a free clinic. So, just as quickly as we got married and I got pregnant, he joined the Army. And since I couldn't afford to stay in our rented flat while he was away at boot camp, I temporarily moved back in with my mother. Considering how upset she was with me for eloping just weeks earlier, I'm surprised she "welcomed" me back at all. Surprised and grateful.

It wasn't all fun and games at first. She didn't waste any time lecturing me about my recent stupid decisions and also predicted that John only joined the service to run away from his responsibilities. *Yeah, like I wouldn't be able to locate him through the U.S. Army.* (Typical of my mother's view on life, she never saw glasses being half-full. I'm pretty sure she never saw them as half-empty either—more like bone dry, with water marks in the bottom from being dried up so long.)

As the days and weeks went by, though, she saw that he called and wrote whenever he could and decided he wasn't all bad. She and I even drove to Ft. Leonard Wood, Missouri for his graduation from boot camp. After that, he was sent to another base for additional training, and I wasn't allowed to join him until he was eligible for housing.

So, more weeks went by. My mother lived in the same tiny, 2nd floor, two-bedroom apartment she and I shared when I was in high school. It was all she could afford, and the walls were thin; but at least it was clean and in a nice area. I was lonesome and bored out of my mind. All my friends were either away at college or had full-time jobs. The only thing I did all day, every day, was sit and watch TV and wait for the mailman to come, hoping for another letter from John. Since the walls were so thin and the

TV stand was next to the front door, I always heard the mailman come in, open up the apartment boxes, and push the mail in. I practically held my breath, waiting to hear the foyer door open and close again, knowing he'd left. Immediately, I'd yank open the door and dash down with mailbox key in hand. *Please, please, please let there be a letter for me today.* Put key in. Turn to right. Lift up door. Alleluia! On those days I received a letter, nothing else mattered. Everything was good in the world and I'd walk back up the stairs with happiness in my heart.

I had an entire routine when reading John's letters: 1. Don't open it right away. 2. Hold it and gaze at it for a few seconds. 3. Place it on the oak coffee table. 4. Walk the ten steps it takes to get into the kitchen and to the refrigerator. 5. Open door, reach in, and grab a Pepsi, and walk back to couch. 6. Bend knees, lower myself down onto couch, reach down and pick up letter. 7. Settle into my seat, take a deep breath—ah, open and read the letter. 8. Then read it again and again and again.

On the days I didn't get a letter, I'd read through all the previous ones and that helped with my disappointment level.

I barely left the apartment except to run errands. I had no money for mall shopping and didn't really need anything at that point, anyway. One afternoon, when Mother rode the city bus to work, I drove her car to the grocery store. As I pulled into a parking spot, I noticed a woman near the entrance door, holding a clipboard with a tablet of paper. *Uh oh, I hope she doesn't ask me to take a survey. I just hate that.* I climbed out of the driver's seat, slammed and locked the car door, and started walking…with my head down and eyes looking the other way.

"Excuse me! Would you mind taking a survey?"

Darn it. Survey Lady wasn't going to allow me to avoid her, was she? I looked up at her smiling face as she started saying something about free coupons. I agreed to answer a couple of short questions. What could it hurt? Saving money was high on my priority list.

I think she asked about products I use in my home. I don't remember anything specific except for my answer to her last question.

"And how many hours a day would you say you watch TV?"

Hmmm. This was going to be easy. Let's see, I watch it from the time I wake up until the time I go to bed at night.

"I'd say I watch TV about 18 hours a day," I replied. She was looking down at her sheet of paper, getting ready to scribble my answer, when my words sunk in. She jerked her head up and stared at me as if I'd spoken in a foreign language.

"Oh, honey, you must've misunderstood me. You can't possibly watch 18 hours of TV a day. Most people say about three or four hours. Doesn't that sound about right to you?"

"Uh, no it doesn't. I know what I do all day long. I sit and watch TV until it's time to go to bed. Oh, except for the time it takes to fix supper for my mother and myself, but I can see the TV from the kitchen, too."

She looked at me in utter disbelief and said, "Well, I'm still going to write down three hours a day because nobody would believe your answer."

Hmm...well so much for an accurate survey and a waste of my precious time.

I walked away from Survey Lady and through the automatic doors into the grocery store. It was then I remembered she didn't give me my free coupons, but I wasn't about to go back and ask for them. She'd already pretty much humiliated me for the entire day, and 10 cent coupons weren't worth nearly enough to add to my embarrassment. I certainly didn't need a stranger to inform me that my life was pathetic. What did she know about being pregnant, alone at home all day waiting for a letter from her husband, far away? I bet she'd watch a zillion hours of TV, too.

From Pigtails to Chin Hairs

Armpit of the USA

Oh, the things you do when you're young, stupid, and believe you're in love, such as riding in a Greyhound bus for over fourteen hours when you're more than just a couple of months pregnant. Yep, that was me. I remember two things about that trip. One was how uncomfortable I was no matter how I tried to sit or stretch out across the seat. The other was that it seemed to take days and days to get through the state of Texas. It made me think of the movie, *Giant*, with Rock Hudson and Elizabeth Taylor. They'd been in their private sleeper car on their honeymoon traveling by train from the Northeast to Texas. Elizabeth's character, Leslie, had been staring out the window for some time.

Leslie Benedict (Elizabeth Taylor): **"Tell me as soon as we're in Texas."**

Jordon Bick Benedick (Rock Hudson): **"That's Texas you're looking at honey, for the last eight hours."**

The bus finally pulled into the station at the army base, let out a loud whoosh of smelly smoke, and came to a stop. I managed to slowly get up and rubbed my lower back, as I peered out the window. Thank goodness John was there with a big smile to greet me. I smiled back and waved—knowing if I had to sit there one more minute, I would've broken down and cried.

Right after I hobbled down the steps and onto the ground, my smile disappeared when John informed me he didn't have the money for a taxi. *Huh? How were we going to get "home?" Couldn't he have borrowed a car? Did he forget that I'm **six months pregnant?***

But he grabbed my suitcase, took my hand, and looked into my eyes with such love I couldn't be mad at him for not having money at that moment, could I? We were still sort-of newlyweds, anyway.

So we walked the couple of miles to our tiny, white bungalow. When we walked in, I obviously noticed it was completely empty; but before I could say or do anything, I asked where the bathroom was and made a mad dash toward it. Whew, what a relief. It was all I could do not to wet my pants while I walked! When I came back out, all I saw was shiny tile floors. (I bet they had twenty layers of wax on them. You know how the Army is—all that spit and shine stuff.) No furniture, no dishes, no air conditioner, no nothin'! All of this during April in El Paso, where it was already beginning a trial run at its summertime sizzle.

We lived on an army base, ironically named Ft. Bliss, right in the heart of El Paso. Now, I'm sure it's a very nice town even if you only possess the bare necessities in life, which we did not. Ft. Bliss was dry, flat, brown, dusty, and hot. There was nothing beautiful or blissful about it. Thus my nickname for it: Armpit of the USA.

The first night I was there, we slept on a sheet on the hard, tile floor. Slept may not be the correct word since I certainly wasn't comfortable and didn't actually sleep much. Let's just say I was in a horizontal position. But things improved in the next couple of days. We acquired a used mattress to lay on the floor of the bedroom (eeeew—a *used* mattress?), then a bed frame, plus an old black and white television set, and a couple of webbed lawn chairs to furnish the living room. Then to finish it all off, we picked up an old wooden desk to use for a kitchen table. Not exactly *House Beautiful*, but what more could a wife and mother-to-be ask from her Private First Class husband? Besides, I was "in love," you know. Oh, and thank goodness, we had a radio. I couldn't live without music.

That summer, 1972, one of the songs I loved was "Taxi" by Harry Chapin. I'd never heard anything so hauntingly beautiful and heartbreakingly sad at the same time. Forty years later, no matter where I am I still get chills the moment I hear those first few notes and that unmistakable voice.

I don't know what I would've done if it hadn't been for our wonderful next door neighbors. The young wife saw me sitting out on our front slab of a porch the second morning I was there. She walked over to introduce herself, probably because I looked so pitiful. There I was a shy, young, Army wife, pregnant and sitting outside on a concrete stoop. I guess it hadn't occurred to me to bring one of our lawn chairs outside to sit on. She asked me to come over later for lunch. Her name was Laura, and what a wonderful gift she gave me: the gift of friendship, especially when I needed it so desperately. I don't think I would've survived that summer of pregnancy and loneliness without her. I practically lived there during the weekdays while our husbands were at work. Their house was identical to ours on the outside, just like all the others in the low ranking soldiers' housing area; but it was actually full of furniture, drapes, and knick knacks. The two most important items there, though, were the wonderfully comfy living room chair and the air cooler—neither of which we had.

My precious baby, Scott, was born that July, and we left Ft. Bliss soon after. Off to new destinations, wherever the Army chose to send us. Next assignment: Germany.

Laura and I kept in touch for a few years after that summer, mostly through Christmas cards. But we both moved too many times, and somehow the mail didn't catch up. One of the last letters I received was full of details about her new, happy marriage. I was so glad for her, but that letter also made me feel all the more sad and helpless about my own life. Military marriages had a dismal survival rate, and mine was definitely in malfunction mode.

I can honestly say a few good things about that "Armpit of the USA" though: It gave me my first taste of military life, which I really enjoyed; taught me how to get by with practically nothing (which I was used to anyway, and that would continue on for many years); showed me the meaning of camaraderie; forced me to mature rather quickly; and presented me with my first son Scott! All this at the ripe old age of nineteen.

Were Those Salad Tongs?

The U.S. Army almost killed my newborn son and me. Actually, it wasn't the entire Army—just a few medical personnel at William Beaumont Hospital in Ft. Bliss, Texas.

It was the end of July 1972, a week before my due date. I was swollen, bloated, and miserable. Our living room "furniture" provided zero comfort, such as it was. Two webbed lawn chairs near the black and white TV were the sum of our décor. My only alternative was to lie on our bed with its saggy, lumpy mattress.

I'd been having sporadic labor pains for a few hours, only minor ones; but when they came closer together, John and I decided to head over to the hospital. I was checked in and escorted to a small room with cement walls painted typical army green. It looked like a jail cell without the bars. A medical person of some sort would come in to check on me from time to time, but nothing much was happening. John was allowed in the room at times; but since neither one of us had reason to be concerned, I told him it was okay to leave for a while.

"Honey, go get something to eat. You don't need to be here right now. Nothing's going on anyway. I wish they'd just send me home."

"Okay," he said, "but I'll be right back. I just need to grab a sandwich and some coffee."

He hadn't needed to rush back because I remained in various stages of labor for hours and hours. Sometimes the pains completely stopped and then intense ones would reappear. A nurse came in at one point with an injection to ease my pain. When checked on a bit later, it was a medic who asked, "Well, Mrs. Jones, did that take care of your labor pain?"

To which I deadpanned, "No, but my entire right leg is numb. Thanks."

You'd think that would've worried me, but I was raised to believe doctors were brilliant and almost god-like. And besides, no one else seemed concerned. And have I mentioned how young, naïve, and trusting I was?

John continued to check on me once in a while; but when he came in all smiles, turned white, gagged, and bolted from the room, I knew I wouldn't see him again until after our baby was born.

"Uh, hey. Bye, honey," was all I could muster.

Later, he told me when he saw blood all over those white sheets, he felt bad for me, and the sight of blood made him queasy. *Hmmm, some soldier he'll be.*

After being in labor off and on for more than14 hours, I finally was wheeled into a delivery room. I couldn't wait to be relieved of my agony and experience childbirth. The only problem with that was by the time I got the spinal, I instantly fell asleep from sheer exhaustion. I woke up briefly to the sensation of my innards being tugged on—a definite pulling, but not painful. Raising my head slightly, I gazed down toward the obstetrician. My vision was blurry, but I thought I saw some tongs, and then my head plopped back down. I had peculiar dreams but at the same time, felt awake and wondered how many hours had gone by and would I ever see my baby. Then a miracle happened. A nurse gently woke me and showed me the most beautiful, little face peeking out from a pastel blue blanket.

"You have a son!"

Looking at him, I realized that with his birth I, too, was reborn. I was no longer a teenage girl but a young mother, experiencing all the emotions of motherhood: cherishing, protecting, and nurturing. But most of all, an abundance of unconditional love. All I could say was, "Ohhhh," knowing my life would never be the same again.

The nurse whisked him off to the nursery, and sometime later, John came to see me. I asked if he had seen our baby yet.

"Isn't he beautiful?" I asked, although it was more of a statement than a question.

To my surprise, he replied, "No! Didn't you see his head and face? His head is all funny shaped because of the forceps they used, and the right side of his face is partially paralyzed."

Oh, that explains those tongs I saw….

"Oh my God! Is he going to be all right? Did you talk to the doctor?"

"Yeah, he said everything will shape up in a couple of days."

I couldn't wait to be able to actually see and hold him. Although we called him Scott, somehow it didn't seem natural referring to such a tiny angel using a "big boy" name. In a couple of months and for the next year, he was Punky, which evolved from, "What a little punkin!"

I had no idea that all the first-time mothers in this hospital had "rooming-in" with their babies, and there didn't seem to be a choice about it either. The philosophy was that mothers who already had children needed their relaxation more than the rest of us did. Imagine my surprise when shortly after I was settled into my room, a nurse rolled in a baby cart. She placed it against the wall, saying, "Here's your son," then closed the door behind her as she walked out.

What? I'd never heard of such a thing. When my older sister had her two babies, they stayed in the nursery. All the newborns in the movies stayed in nurseries, too. What was I supposed to do? I'd read books all through my pregnancy and felt ready to be the best mother in the world. But I'd hoped to have a couple of days of sleep before I went home with my bundle of joy. What if he had colic? I immediately started an internal litany of prayers that my baby would *not* have colic.

During the first 24 hours, my plan about sleeping went right out the window. Scott wasn't colicky, but he did cry and fuss a lot. I felt helpless and at fault and didn't know what to do besides the rocking, back patting, diaper changing, and bottle feeding. After calling the nurses for help a few times and their awareness of the crying (Scott's—not mine), one of them came in and said, "Honey, you just have to get some sleep, so we'll take care of your baby. We'll bring him back when it's feeding time." She grabbed hold of the cart and rolled my son out. The minute my head hit the pillow, I was out. I didn't wake up until the next morning when a different nurse came in to give me a few horse pills to choke down.

I always had a dreadful time swallowing any kind of pills, and I blame both of my older sisters for that little phobia. When I was a little girl, I used to watch each of them stand in front of the bathroom mirror, trying to swallow aspirin. (No easy downing of gel caps because they hadn't been invented yet. And why the heck did they stand in front of a mirror, watching themselves?) Geez, it was hard work! It took at least one full glass of water, but most times needed a refill and more sipping. Along with that was the throwing their heads back, in hopes of forcing the already melting, icky, chalky tasting culprit to move on down the throat. It was like propaganda. I'd seen and heard the ordeal enough times to know that "Taking Pills is Hard to Do."

So, when the nurse brought in four huge pills and a one-inch tall Dixie cup containing one sip of water in it, I knew there was going to be a big problem. I'm sure I had a strange look on my face as I looked over the situation.

"What are all these pills for?" I asked.

"To dry up your milk since you're not breast feeding and other vitamins you need," she replied.

"Oh. Well, I'm going to need a lot more water. Milk would even be better."

I'd at least learned over the years that taking pills with milk worked better. I guess it was the thickness of it and maybe also because it was so cold. Water was just too "thin and warm," and tablets immediately dissolved.

"Okay, honey, I'll bring you some milk with your supper then. How about that?" she asked.

"That would be great. Thank you."

When baby Scott was brought back to my room, I loved having him with me. He was so sweet, cute, and good-natured after that first night; my motherly tenderness kicked in and never left.

When the nurse came in with my supper, she brought two cartons of milk, more pills, and asked, "Honey, have you had your bowel movement today?"

I had a history of constipation long before pregnancy and didn't even know what "regular" was.

"Oh, gosh no. I haven't gone in about two weeks." *Other than the enema I was given when I arrived, thank you very much.* Well, you would've thought I just said something completely crazy.

"WHAT? Oh, honey, you need to take some stool softeners. You need to empty your bowels right away and every day."

"Really? I didn't know that. I never go every day. What's a stool softener?"

"I'll go get some, and I'll bring a new carton of milk, too."

Oh great. Another horse pill, and this time she stood and watched as I gulped and gagged and swallowed two of them.

"Those should work fairly quickly. So when you feel the urge to go, you should hurry to the bathroom."

Did I mention I didn't have a bathroom in my room? One of the shared ones was quite a distance down the hall. Wonderful.

Little did I know that because of the difficult birth and the use of forceps, the doctor had either made an incision and/or my skin ripped. After my third day in the hospital and after a problem I had in the restroom when the stool softeners kicked in, I discovered my stitches ruptured.

My obstetrician finally dropped in to see how I was doing, and he verified the problem. Since the old hospital was being closed for good on Friday of that week, he said I would be released, but had to come back to the new hospital on Monday to get my stitches re-sewn. Something that would probably be referred to today as "a little procedure." I just looked at it as a little inconvenience and wasn't concerned.

John came to get Scott and me on that Friday. On one shoulder hung my purse, and on the other was the diaper bag carrying the usual items, plus one blow-up butt donut. I had a feeling it was going to be a long weekend.

~ ~ ~

Monday morning, I was admitted into the brand new hospital. It was built right next door to the old one, but it stood worlds apart. This one looked like a real hospital—clean and sparkly—as opposed to the other, resembling a really old army barracks, which I think it was.

Thank goodness for my next-door neighbor and best friend, Laura, because she helped take care of Scott for us. John could take off a couple of hours once in a while, but mostly had to work. He, of course, kept Scott at night and woke up with him for his bottle feedings. Nothing like a little father-son nurturing right off the bat.

It's odd that I don't remember why none of my family was there to help me, especially my mother. She worked full time, though, and maybe couldn't take any days off. Neither of my two older sisters came either. And there's always the possibility I didn't want any of my family to see how I was living—in a bare house.

My brother, Mike, always used to say he was the black sheep of the family. I never knew exactly why he said it, but I guessed he was kidding. I'm quite sure, though, I definitely carried that label for a number of years.

I'll never forget what I went through during this second admission and what the outcome was. I was prepped for surgery in the usual manner; hospital gown, IV, some kind of pain treatment, and brief information about what was going to happen. Then I was rolled down hallways, in and out of elevators, and into the operating room. Someone leaned over and told me to start counting backwards from 100, and I think I made it to 98.

After waking up in post-op, I was drowsy but relieved and just wanted to go home. That was the last time for a couple of years that I felt any relief either physically or emotionally concerning my stitches.

The surgeon explained that the area, between two important parts of my anatomy, was too small and couldn't be sewn. It would just have to heal by itself. That meant I was left with a not-so-small open gap that would *eventually* close up on its own.

We women learn to rid ourselves of any self-consciousness and modesty when we're pregnant—all those doctor visits, all the medical personnel before, during, and after delivery who peek at and/or examine us. *Well,* I must've been the number one specimen for doctors or pre-med students to observe. Groups of three or more would stroll into my hospital room, ask my permission to see "it" for their learning purposes, and proceed to lift my sheet. Then looks of shock and compassion accompanied the medical terms spoken by the Head Doctor Dude. Then, off they'd go, and I'd be alone until the next group promenaded in.

Even at nineteen, my naivety was beginning to wane and I kept thinking that *some kind* of procedure should be able to be performed!

The day I was released, I got dressed and waited for John to come and get me out of that place. Before he arrived, though, four doctors (or some of them were lawyers?) came into my room. I was given oral and written instructions:

A) Take sitz baths X times a day (which took some creativity since we only had a shower stall in our tiny home).

B) Use a heat lamp X times a day (which we also didn't have, so I used a small desk lamp).

C) Take extreme caution when wiping. *Oh, ya think?*

D) Continue to sit on the butt donut for the next couple of months (or the rest of my life.)

The real kicker though was when I was handed a pen and told to sign my name on a particular line.

"What's this for?" I asked.

"Oh, it's just an affidavit stating that when you have more children, you should have them by C-section," replied one casually.

"Well, that's no problem," I grumbled, as I scribbled my signature on the paper, "because I'm NEVER going to have any more children. Not after what I've been through!"

I think I also heard something about not holding any of them responsible for anything that happened to me and/or to Scott. *Huh?* It was too late; I'd already signed the paper, and besides what good would it do to try to sue the U.S. Army? I wasn't *that* young and naïve!

~~~

I was definitely telling the truth that day because I never wanted to go through that again. I didn't get pregnant until 15 years later, when my second husband, Ron, and I received a very special gift. I became a new mother again in 1987, with the birth of my second son, Mark. And he came into this world by a scheduled C-section!

On the Wings of Love

After I was certain Scott was sleeping peacefully, I tried to settle myself comfortably in the seat next to him. My heart swelled with love as I gazed over at him. What a beautiful face! What had I done to deserve having him in my life? I took a couple of deep breaths and looked out the window into the vast darkness, only to see my own reflection. I was leaving home again. But this time it wasn't by car or bus. I was sitting in a window seat on a Pan Am 747 flying across the Atlantic Ocean.

The jet had taken off from New York's JFK Airport, heading for Heathrow Airport in London, England. There I would be ushered through customs, change planes for the third time, and fly into Frankfurt, Germany. My young, military husband would be anxiously awaiting our arrival. The three of us would then travel a small distance by train to end this extremely long trip. We'd finally be home, at least what would be home for the next twelve months.

I was nineteen years old, traveling alone with Scott, my three-month-old son; and I had absolutely no misgivings. I was too innocent to have the sense to be worried or afraid. I was just doing what came naturally. I was married, I had a new baby, and wherever my military husband went, I obviously followed.

I leaned back against my seat, closed my eyes, and thought about the past few hours. My flight from St. Louis to New York was on TWA and was smooth and uneventful. I innocently assumed the next portion of my lengthy voyage would continue the same way. It never occurred to me I might have any problems. After all, what could possibly go wrong? I'd flown before, maybe not this far or with a baby, but how hard could it be? After exiting the plane at JFK, though, I realized how wrong I was to assume anything.

After getting off the plane and walking into the immense passageway, I wasn't able to find my departing gate. I thought I would have plenty of time since I had a layover, but I had no idea JFK was so enormous. Pan Am flights weren't even listed on any of the several nearby arrival and departure signs. I began to feel as if I was in the *Twilight Zone*, although I knew that was ridiculous. I knew who and where I was. I was Becky Jones, a young wife, a new mother, and I was living in good old 1972.

After aimlessly wandering around too long without asking for help, I finally noticed an airport employee.

"Can you tell me where the Pam Am information is? I haven't been able to find anything about it."

He looked at me with a tired, haggard face and said, "You'll have to board one of the shuttle buses to get to that section."

He pointed the other direction and said I would find the bus there. *What?!* For the first time, panic set in as I hurried to find and board the right bus. I had no idea what would happen if I missed my flight to England, and I certainly didn't want to find out!

After bouncing along for what seemed like hours, the driver finally pulled over by the Pan Am concourse. I carefully stepped down from the bus, walked inside the terminal, and located a sign indicating my flight number. I quickly determined my gate was as far away as possible, noting my location on the "You Are Here" sign.

During the entire time, I held Scott in the infant seat of those days; a baby carrier without handles. The only way to carry it was to place both arms underneath it, slightly bent at the elbows, and hold it in front of your body about waist high. As I trudged along the endless aisles and corridors, I began to lose all feeling in both arms. I had to stop from time to time, set the carrier on the floor, shake my arms, and rearrange my purse and diaper bag over opposite shoulders. I was short and slender and must've been carrying a fourth of my weight.

People passed and jostled me from both directions. No one had time to stop and help a young mother who was obviously struggling. Thankfully, Scott was such a sweet baby. He either slept or smiled the entire time, and I spoke gentle, reassuring words to him, although I was the one needing reassurance.

Just when I thought I'd collapse, a kind looking woman seemed to materialize out of nowhere and came to my aid.

"My goodness," she said. "You've got your hands full there, don't you?"

"Oh, yes ma'am, I do," I replied.

"May I help you carry some of your things?"

I gratefully accepted her offer and declared my sincere thanks. She gently took the diaper bag from one of my arms, which by then had become numb and tingly. She *oohed* and *aahed* over my darling baby boy and remarked what a precious little angel he was. As we walked side by side, we talked about being mothers, traveling with children, and other small talk. I obviously noticed her accent and enjoyed listening to her. We also realized we were heading for the same gate. That's where our similarities ended, though. She was returning to her country, and I was leaving mine.

After we boarded the gigantic jet, I thanked her profusely, and then we lost sight of each other. I thought about the way she had lovingly described Germany: its cities and small towns, delightful architecture, and vast countryside.

I opened my eyes and looked at my watch. How many time zones would I fly through before I arrived? I glanced out the window one more time and then shifted myself around a little, so I could keep my eyes on Scott, who (at the moment) seemed to be drifting back to sleep. I couldn't fight my exhaustion any longer. I dreamed about the next day: the landings, the takeoffs, the boarding, and exiting of planes. Every day was a journey, a passage of time from innocence to maturity.

From Pigtails to Chin Hairs

Episodes in a German Sitcom

Most of my first marriage was spent living in Germany. Those years were filled with countless memories and an assortment of emotions. Not in any particular order: loneliness, shyness, contentment, love, friendship, camaraderie, happiness, anger, nervousness, hurt, and fear.

I made the decision years ago that I would not focus on the bad things. I didn't want to even remember them, let alone spend any valuable time and energy thinking about "what ifs" and "should haves" or any other negative theories. And so, I'll share some of my favorite memories from the two different tours of duty John and I spent there. "Favorite" doesn't necessarily mean "happy."

The first German apartment we lived in was brand new, which would've been really nice, had its design not been so bizarre. I'd never seen anything like it, nor have I since. I remember thinking, *Is this the way all apartment buildings in Germany are built?* It was beyond my comprehension.

The outside of the two-story apartment building consisted of light colored bricks and large windows. I could tell it'd been built recently and began to share John's excitement about our new home. He held open the all-glass front door, I wheeled Scott in his stroller through the entry, and we walked into a large foyer. I noticed there were six separate doors.

"Which one is our apartment?" I asked, feeling enthusiastic.

John replied, "Well, four of those doors go into our rooms!"

Huh? Our rooms? Go into our rooms?

"What do you mean?"

"Well, that door there," as he pointed to the one on the left, "that's our kitchen. And the one to the right of it is our living room. Now, that next one goes into Sergeant Smith's bedroom, and—"

"WHAT?" I practically screamed. "What are you talking about? What kind of apartment is this, anyway?!"

"Now, hold on. Let me finish. Now, as I was saying . . . the next door after Sarge's room, is *our* bedroom. Let's go in, and you can unpack your suitcases."

"But where's our bathroom?" I was afraid to hear the answer.

"Well, that's the only kind of bad thing about the apartment. We share the bathroom with Sarge." He mumbled that last sentence, but I was sure of what I heard.

"WHAT?!" This time I didn't practically scream—I screamed.

As I stood in disbelief, still trying to survey the situation and let it all sink in, John walked over and opened all of *our* doors. First, the kitchen. He opened the door in grand fashion, raising and

144

waving his other arm giving me the old game show model routine. It was really tiny, but at least the place was furnished with cabinets, a table, and a couple of chairs. (Cabinets and closets were not built in, as in the U.S.) He performed the same routine with each door opening. Tiny living room, and ancient furniture. Large bedroom had a bed, dresser, and baby crib. Boy, the Army spared no expense when it came to furnishing a low-ranking soldier's apartment. Everything looked like it just fell off Sanford and Son's truck.

"Okay, let me get this straight. When I want to walk from **our** bedroom to **our** kitchen, I have to walk out into **this** foyer, with its big, glass door. AND if it's in the night when I have to warm up a bottle for Scott, I'll be in my jammies. What if I run into Sarge? AND what if I have to get up in the middle of the night to use the bathroom, and Sarge is in there, *using it?*"

"Well, I don't know," John said, shaking his head, as if he'd never thought of that. Leave it to a man.

There was one good thing about the entire situation, and I use that term loosely. We didn't have to share the kitchen. There's no way I would've shared a refrigerator with a stranger. No. Freakin'. Way.

Speaking of kitchens, that was in early November of 1972, and I don't remember a thing about Thanksgiving that year. I don't remember if I'd made any friends yet. I don't know if we ate turkey TV dinners at our apartment or had dinner at the mess hall. And obviously, since it's an American holiday, there were no decorations in town. It continues to be the worst and loneliest Thanksgiving of my life, which is saying a lot, because the first, second, third, etc., after my dad left were difficult and unhappy ones, too.

Scott being only three months old still took lots of naps and obviously didn't talk. I was terribly homesick and lonesome during the day while John was at work. We had no radio, no TV, no stereo. One of the truly pitiful things I did to entertain myself while Scott napped was listening to his teddy bear music box, over and over and over. Can you imagine? I don't remember what song it played; thank goodness that memory hasn't lingered. But I can see myself sitting at our small kitchen table, winding it up and listening to it play for its few short minutes, then the gradual slowing down: plink, plink, plink.

It's a wonder I didn't go nuts! (Oh yeah, I forgot. Mother said I already was.) I *had* to have some kind of noise to force the unending silence away. We had no telephone, either, but that wouldn't have done me any good. I didn't know anyone to call. Long distance calls at that time cost a fortune, so that ruled out any possibility of calling friends or family back in the States.

We lived in a tiny town with beautiful sidewalks and quaint, little shops, just a few miles from the small army post, and I could've easily gone for walks pushing Scott in a stroller. I was extremely shy, though, and I didn't venture out during the day those first months we were there. I wished we lived in housing, where I would've been surrounded by other military wives; but housing was limited, and John was only a private first class and not even eligible.

I don't remember how long it was before I had any friends, but it seems like it was only a couple of months. Soon I met Debbie, the wife of one of John's Army buddies and our instant friendship never waned. We've written to each other, sent Christmas cards, and even talked on the phone a few times ever since those long ago days.

From Pigtails to Chin Hairs

The Tupperware Queen of Tacoma, Washington

We left Ft. Bliss when Scott was only six weeks old. His first plane trip was from El Paso, Texas to St. Louis, where my mother still lived. John left a few days after we got there since he had to report to his new assignment: West Germany. I was excited about going, but also sad about leaving family and friends for an entire year. We wouldn't see or talk to anyone in the States for a long time. Writing and receiving letters in the mail was such a treat.

Once John found a furnished apartment for us, about six weeks later, Scott and I flew across the Atlantic Ocean together. What a voyage! We enjoyed our time there and met some wonderful people, both Americans and Germans. But not having much spending money kept us from doing any traveling; and I've said for years that someday I'm going back, when I can really afford it.

When his year was up, John's new assignment was Ft. Lewis, Washington, near Tacoma. I wasn't thrilled about living there, all that rain and all. In fact, we were there for at least a month until we had a beautiful, sunny day and I realized I could see Mt. Rainier right outside our bedroom window!

We arrived in St. Louis from Germany the same way we left—with just the clothes on our backs and whatever was in our three suitcases, plus our one year old son, of course! We bought an old, green Buick with an overloaded odometer, attached a U-Haul trailer on the back, and headed to the Great Northwest in the middle of January. This time we had a crib, stroller, baby clothes, toys, and a few pieces of furniture and household goods. You could say I was slightly nervous about the drive: all that snow, ice, and sliding rocks on mountain roads. The trip really wasn't too bad, though, and we made it in one piece.

Following my husband all over the world didn't bother me one bit. It was what wives did, especially military wives. I was still a shy young woman, though, particularly when living in new areas and not knowing anyone. Fortunately, most seasoned military wives were outgoing because they knew we were all in the same boat. I just needed to mature and have some confidence in myself. I knew I was a good wife and a wonderful mother. I loved Scott more than anything in the world, and I prided myself on how well I took care of him. I was so thankful for having him in my life, especially during my homesickness and loneliness, and those times when John would get so angry. I don't know if it took a couple of years for his temper to really show itself or if the stress of the Army caused him to have emotional swings. At times, we seemed so happy; and then all of a sudden, he'd scream at me about the littlest thing—and each time, I was totally taken off-guard. For example, when we got home from shopping at the commissary one day, he told me to wash the dirty dishes I'd left in the sink that morning.

"Oh, there's only a couple of plates, bowls, and silverware. I'll do them later," was my reply. He became outraged, picked up one of the heavy, stoneware plates, and hurled it against the back kitchen door, breaking it into pieces.

He then screamed at me as he picked up another plate, "When I tell you to do something, you better do it, and I mean NOW!"

"Stop it! Don't break anything else! I'll wash them right now. I'm sorry." I started crying and Scott looked frightened, too.

John sat down to watch TV, lit a cigarette and plopped his feet on top of the coffee table as if nothing happened. I cried silently as I quickly washed up the dishes, put them and the groceries away, and cleaned up the broken dish mess on the floor. I was the one who always apologized after these kinds of incidents, knowing it hadn't really been my fault at all. But I did it to "keep peace," attempting to have a good marriage, and keep Scott and myself safe from any physical abuse.

One evening I was invited by one of the neighborhood wives to a Tupperware party and I had a great time. I think I bought one inexpensive container since we never had any extra money. It wasn't because we spent it carelessly either. We took care of our bills first, then food and diapers, and normally had just enough left for gas for our one car.

Remember that ancient typewriter I mentioned in the crowbar chapter? It came along with us to Washington and was the one thing we could hock every month when we needed ten bucks. Yes, ten bucks was what we got from the pawn shop for it; and then after payday, we'd go back and pick it up again. One month, we finally either didn't have the money to get it back or forgot about it because it didn't come along with us when we left Ft. Lewis.

Back to the party. The hostess was actually in training and the district manager Tupperware lady, Ruth, was doing the presentation. Then she did her spiel about how we could make money and get lots of free Tupperware if we joined her team. Why in the world I thought I could do that— I have no idea. Obviously the real me was either in denial or hiding inside, longing to come out and show herself. Whoever I was at that moment, I signed up.

Ruth came with me on my first couple of parties. She also picked me up on her way to the weekly Monday morning sales meetings. It was something like I'd never seen before. A large roomful of Tupperware ladies, and a couple of Tupperware men, were whipped into a selling frenzy in a very short period of time. There was whooping and hollering and awards handed out. It was quite mesmerizing. I even received a crown-shaped pin, made from rhinestones, because I had a big dollar amount party. After my first meeting, I was ready to go out and conquer the Greater Tacoma area. That is until I got back home, walked through the front door of our little apartment, and my real life smacked me in my face. I was just a housewife and a mother, and

I really loved being that person. But I wanted to succeed, and I also wanted to sell enough to be able to keep my demo Tupperware products. So one day, I got up the nerve to do one of the things the sales meetings promised would work: cold calling from the White Pages. Every time I even considered it, my knees got weak, my stomach felt sick, and my hands got clammy; but that day— I knew I had to do it. Opening the pantry door, I pulled out the large Seattle/Tacoma White Pages and plopped it on the kitchen table.

Okay. You can do this. Quit being such a baby. Just do it! With my eyes closed, I flipped open the heavy book, turned a few pages, and plunked my finger down on a name: Smith. Okay. Good. Now I had a name and a phone number. *Just pick up the phone, Becky, and make that call.* I walked over to the wall phone, picked up the receiver, and dialed the lucky number. After three rings, a woman's voice said, "Hello."

"Hello, Mrs. Smith. My name is Becky Jones, and I'm a Tupperware representative in Tacoma—"

"How'd you get this phone number?" she snapped.

"Well, ma'am I found it in the White Pages and —"

"Oh no, you didn't! This is an unlisted number, and I don't know how you people keep getting it and calling me and....."

"I'm very sorry, Mrs. Smith, but....."

"What's your name again? I'm going to call the authorities."

"Uh, sorry. I have to hang up now." Click.

Oh my god. That woman was nuts!

I quickly closed up the phone book and put it back in the pantry. I never made another cold call, and that was the day I lost any desire to become The Tupperware Queen of Tacoma, Washington.

At least I did manage to keep all my fabulous, free Tupperware. That was almost 40 years ago; and somehow, during our various moves across the country and across the ocean, bowls and lids were either given away, left behind, or lost. I'm happy to say that I still have my blue canister set, and I use them, because they work great, keeping everything airtight. And in case I ever need to feel like a queen, I even have that dazzling crown-shaped pin that I can wear at any time.

Doris Day, AE Hotchner, and Me

During the bleakest moments in my first marriage, I came across a paperback book, which contained poignant and inspirational words. No, it wasn't a bible or other religious periodical. It also wasn't written by or about a renowned motivational speaker, legendary sports figure, or high-flying astronaut. It was a biography: *Doris Day: Her Own Story*, by AE Hotchner.

The year was 1976. John and I and our four-year-old son, Scott, were living in Germany again. It was his second tour there, and this time it was for three, long years. I'm so thankful that once again, just like when we lived at Ft. Bliss, I was fortunate to be best friends with the army wife next door. I don't know how I would've gotten through such stressful times if it hadn't been for her and her friendship.

When we married, I honestly believed I would have the Happily Ever After marriage I'd always dreamed of (most likely because I was so young and naïve); and even though I married a guy I'd been dating for *one* month, I truly thought it would last.

But somehow, someone got in the way of that happiness—John himself. He became more and more controlling, obsessive, demeaning, and I didn't know why. I don't know if he disliked his job or disliked me; but whatever it was, we weren't a happy couple. We lived on the eighth floor of a high-rise apartment building, used strictly for Army housing. Sometimes when hearing beautiful love songs while listening to the Armed Forces radio station, I'd stare out those windows and think about my life. I especially remember crying during John Denver's "Annie's Song," and Dave Loggins' "Please Come to Boston." I so wanted to be loved like the women in those songs.

Supper *had* to be on the table at 5:00 pm when he walked in from work: meat, potatoes, and vegetables. If he wasn't home by 5:15, I knew he wouldn't be there until sometime after midnight. Most of the food was wasted. I was angry and hurt. He and his buddies were out drinking…again

Every time this happened, Scott and I would play with his toys as I pretended to be my usual happy mommy self, while pacing back and forth peeking out the living room windows. One minute I'd be thinking, *Dear God, please let him get home in one piece;* but in the next breath, *I'm going to strangle him when he gets home for doing this to me again and again and again.*

In Germany in the mid-70s, none of us military families had phones. They were much too expensive. So, I couldn't call anywhere to check on him, and of course, he couldn't call me. (That was always one of his favorite excuses. "But honey, if I could've called, you know I would have.") Like hell, he would have.

I never knew when his temper would flare, and he'd yell at me and/or Scott. When he got home from work, besides wanting his supper on the table, our apartment had to be clean and uncluttered. Sometimes he actually gave it the old white-glove treatment while I held my breath, hoping it was up to par. I turned into a timid, little mouse, afraid I might say or do the wrong thing. I desperately wanted to leave, taking Scott with me of course, but we couldn't exactly jump on a bus and head home. Home was an ocean away.

It was during that period I bought the authorized biography. When I was growing up, I'd loved Doris Day and wanted to be just like her. I assumed her real life was just like her happy movie lives. I was shocked and saddened when I read about her childhood and her abusive first marriage. Every scene and situation, every quote, every word encouraged me. I knew I'd find a way out. I just needed a plan.

In 1998, a lifetime after I'd left John, I decided to write to Ms. Day (or as I like to call her, "Doris"). I'd always thought about writing and yet also thought it was silly. She wouldn't have time to acknowledge all her fan letters, would she? But I did want to thank her and let her know that her story had made such an impact on my life. I had no mailing address for her, but I knew she lived in Carmel, California…or had at one time. I sent a handwritten note to her, stamped, and with my return address, of course (in case it couldn't be delivered). I addressed it something like this:

> Ms. Doris Day – Movie Star & Dog Lover
> Carmel, CA. 93923

I looked up the zip code for Carmel, California, and there were three. I chose one of them, for no particular reason, hoping my note would reach her. Well, would you believe she not only received it, but she responded? Can you say, "*THRILLED*"?

I've guarded her reply note, envelope included, with my life ever since then!

DORIS DAY

March 5, 1998

Becky Povich
XXXXXXXXXXXXX
XXXXXXXXXXXXX

Dear Becky,

Congratulations – good move and I'm very proud of you!!

It thrills me to know that my autobiography gave you the courage to do what you did and of course, hearing from someone like you makes it all so worthwhile. To know that I helped you really gives me great joy and I appreciate so very much your sharing your thoughts with me.

Take care of yourself, Becky, don't get into trouble again!

Love,

Doris Day

Almost a decade after that, I had the opportunity to meet the fabulous author himself, Mr. AE

Hotchner, when he gave a presentation in 2007 at his alma mater, Washington University in St. Louis. He's led such an amazing life and had been good friends with Ernest Hemingway. During his speech that evening, he donated huge stacks of Hemingway's handwritten letters, and if my memory is correct, also some handwritten chapters of a book or two.

Afterwards, there were Hotchner books to buy and I bought an armful of them. As I waited to see him, I thought about what I would say when I finally made it to the book signing table. I was the last person in line, and the ushers were getting a bit pushy. Although I was loaded down with his books, the only one I placed on the table in front of him was the yellowed, paperback copy I'd kept all these years. I'll never forget the look on his face when he lifted his eyes to mine. As I was being practically shoved along, I blabbered all in one breath, "Mr. Hotchner, I bought this book shortly after it came out in the 1970s, and I was in an abusive marriage at that time. And it gave me the courage to leave. You saved my life! You and Doris Day saved my life. Thank you so much!"

He signed it and handed it back with puzzled, yet kind eyes. Hopefully, he might remember that evening and realize just how much his writing meant to one woman—the woman with the much loved, dog-eared Doris Day biography.

Getting Away

When John and I split up, it was during his second tour in Germany. It wasn't that I thought I didn't love him anymore. In fact, I didn't know how I felt about him. I do know I'd become intimidated by his mood swings, which happened even when he didn't drink. Many times, I was afraid of saying or doing the wrong thing. Weird. It was similar to being around my mother after she and my dad divorced—walking on eggshells, not wanting to upset things. But in her case, I didn't suffer from any abuse, just an emotionally hollow mother at times.

Looking back all these years later, it was almost as if he was jealous of me and disliked me for maturing intellectually. Did he want me to stay the 18-year-old he married? Was it because I had a girlfriend or two that I was close to? He'd already accused them of "putting ideas into my head." You know, those 1970's opinions about women being real people and having the right to be themselves. Yeah, those crazy ideas. I *had* begun to stand up to him at times, when I felt it was safe.

One day, I decided I wanted a new hair style and color. I was tired of my dishwater brown hair and also the length of it. I think John wanted me to keep it the way it was, but I thought I'd look sort of cute with a pixie-cut and also an auburn color.

One of the wives I knew in our building was a hair stylist and offered to cut and color it for me. My self-esteem at that time was about as low as it could get, and I just knew this would give me a real boost.

When I saw myself in the mirror, I couldn't believe it. That was me? Hey, I was cute, wasn't I? I felt on top of the world and hoped John would also think I looked good. He walked in shortly afterwards and when he opened his mouth, my "boost" was totally deflated.

"Honey, how do you like my hair?" I asked, smiling and twirling so he could see the full effect.

"It looks like shit," was his response. He was in his Army fatigues, just like any other work day, but the scowl on his face seemed even more foreboding.

It's not as if our entire five and a half years of marriage, was horrible. We had lots of good, fun times mostly with other American couples we knew. We played thousands of games of Pinochle and Spades. I had an awful time holding all those Pinochle cards! I don't remember anything about the rules, but I think 13 cards were dealt to each person. I can still see and hear the guys snapping their cards down on the kitchen table and their rambunctious comments as they trumped the hand. We usually played the wives against the husbands. It was more fun, and we wouldn't get glared at for playing the wrong card. Those were really great times.

John was close to being transferred again, and since our marriage was unraveling, I talked him into letting Scott and me go home a couple of months ahead of him, to get settled. I think he actually knew the real reason I wanted to leave, but we didn't talk about it and I didn't want to make any waves. He filled out the necessary paperwork and received the two plane tickets, which were for a couple of weeks later. Because of that, I kept them in my purse, just in case I needed to make a quick exit.

It so happened that I did need to leave before those two weeks were up. Scott and I spent our last few days in Germany at the apartment of Army friends in a nearby town. John exploded one evening when he came home from work and found an insignificant amount of sand on our balcony. Yep, Sand.On.Our.Balcony. Not on the floor inside our apartment. Nope. Scott and I had been down at the playground and we both got sand in our shoes. We'd carefully walked straight from the front door to the balcony, which was located outside our master bedroom, and emptied our shoes out there.

He had a fit, so I immediately grabbed a broom and swept the sand off the balcony, down the eight stories to the ground below. I began to get that sick feeling, the one I always got when he was irrational and/or drunk. I took the broom back into the kitchen closet as he followed. He then yelled at me about being such a horrible housewife. I knew from his previous outbursts that this time was different. It didn't seem to matter whether I tried to "explain" anything or tried to calm him down with promises of trying harder.

As I walked back into our bedroom, he grabbed me by my upper arms, lifted me, and flung me onto our bed. I don't remember if he said anything at that moment, but that's when I knew I had to get away from him. I took my purse from the dresser, grabbed Scott from his room and got the hell out of there.

I held Scott's hand as we hurried along the two miles to the army post, straight to the military police office. I have no idea what my exact words were to my little son because I was intent on getting away safely. But I know I reassured him in words his sweet, four-year-old brain could understand.

As we walked into the headquarters, I started talking to the MPs before they could say a word. Large bruises were already visible on my upper arms, as I explained the situation, barely taking a breath.

"My husband just went into a rage, grabbed my arms, threw me on the bed, and that's how I got these bruises! Will you please come back with me so I can pack a suitcase? I already have plane tickets for my little boy and me to go back to the States. I'm afraid to go back and get my things, though."

They calmed me down somewhat, gave both Scott and me some water to drink, and examined the plane tickets I showed them.

Scott stayed at the MP office with the desk clerk as the two I'd spoken to drove me to my apartment building. After the three of us rode the elevator up to the eighth floor, and walked to my door, I realized I'd held my breath the entire time. But when John opened the door and saw two very tall, muscular military police officers, the look on his face went from anger, to intimidated, in just seconds. I was finally able to breathe.

The MPs stood between John and me as I grabbed a suitcase and threw random items of clothing I'd pulled from drawers and the closet. Then I went into Scott's room and did the same thing. I was finished and ready to leave in what felt like mere seconds.

During my mad rush, the officers questioned John about my bruises and I knew then and there that I'd never forget the words that came out of his mouth.

"Now, let me ask you this," he said, "How would you like it if you came home and there was sand all over the balcony and you didn't have any clean socks?"

Yep, that about summed up the situation.

I detected sympathetic looks from the MPs and the three of us walked out the door. For the first time in months, I felt safe, and although I didn't know then that it would take years for me to regain my self-confidence, I definitely knew I was doing the right thing for myself and for Scott.

Becky and Ron's wedding day 1983

Part V:

A NEW LIFE BACK IN THE STATES

From Pigtails to Chin Hairs

An Airport, Two Old Ladies, and Special Footprints

The last time I saw my sister Jo Ann, it was 1984, just days before she died. After receiving the news from her husband that we needed to get there right away to say our goodbyes, many family members flew to Miami/Ft. Lauderdale from different parts of the country: Iowa, Missouri, and Georgia. She was in their living room in a convalescent bed and each one of us spent hours alone with her, while others slept in shifts. Someone was always by her side, whether she wanted to talk or rest or sleep. I think most of us were in denial. I know I was. How could she be dying? She looks fine. Her hair is growing back since the chemo ended. She makes perfect sense when she talks. This just cannot be happening! She's only 46 years old!

And because I was in denial, I didn't say all the things I wanted to say; but at least, I did tell her I loved her. I should've told her how much she meant to me and how much fun I always had with her (even when she was being the "big sister" and bossing me around!) I admired her so much. She was the single, working woman, making it by herself in the

169

corporate world—an office interior decorator. She was the Doris Day character I loved in the movies. She was well dressed, intelligent, funny, and had a great figure. She dated somewhat, but no one could measure up to her standards. That was until one day, when a special guy came along. Outwardly, he didn't appear anything like the kind of man Jo Ann would be interested in, but somehow, he broke through that wall of her perfectionism and she fell in love. Thank God she and Jason met. She was really happy those last six years . . . SIX YEARS.

Everyone said it was a blessing she never had children. They would've been left motherless. People were always looking for "blessings" in these situations. The only real blessing I could think of would be that she had never gotten cancer in the first place. How's that for a blessing?

We held hands during my last evening with her. We both shed a few semi-silent tears. I knew there were unspoken words, hanging in the air above both of us that neither could say. At one point, she visibly began to cry as she told me she always loved me, even when I was a little girl, and she was so jealous of me. I looked at her in disbelief, as she sobbed silently, and I tried to console and shush her. Why in the world was she ever jealous of me? Well, I was kind of spoiled and pouted a lot when I was itty-bitty. Looking back, I wish we would've talked in greater length about so many different things. Again, I blame it on my refusal to accept her impending death. I'd never been summoned like that before. I was going through the motions, but none of it felt real.

My plane reservation was for the next day, but I didn't want to leave. I could've easily changed flights. Others were still staying, yet I was told to go on home—there was no need for me to stay.

(You know how you get through certain situations in life, and don't remember some of the basic things? But you do remember silly details, like the color of a chair. That's pretty much how I existed throughout the months before Jo Ann's death. Somehow, I would get out of bed every morning, get myself dressed, and cry as I drove to work.)

That's how that next morning was. Someone drove me to the airport and dropped me off at the outside baggage check. I think it may have been my brother, Mike, but I really have no idea. That part was just a blur. I knew I was leaving my sister for the final time, and it was too painful to acknowledge. Whoever it was, we hugged goodbye.

I checked my bag at the Eastern Airline counter, was handed the suitcase tag number, and found my way to the correct gate. I had quite a wait before boarding the plane, and all I could do was cry. Right out in the open, while sitting on a turquoise blue, plastic chair, in front of hundreds of travelers. Most of them had fantastic tans, like in the commercials: Coppertone, Sea & Ski, and Ban de Soleil. (Jo Ann always slathered on sun tan oil when she was younger, always trying to get that perfect tan. That scent and the smell of cigarettes always takes me back to her.) Some of the people wore flip-flops, and almost all of them looked like they couldn't be happier. I watched as people bustled by. It was June in southern Florida and many were obviously on vacation. There were families, kids, laughter, diaper bags, souvenirs, etc.

In the midst of it all, I cried openly, clutching my purse on my lap, reaching into it and grabbing tissues, one after another. I felt like a drippy faucet at first, trying to disguise my crying. Then it became impossible as all the memories and "what-ifs" came flooding out. I didn't care if anyone noticed me, and at the same time, I kind of felt as if I was invisible. It never occurred to me that anyone would walk up and speak to me. I assumed people would see that I was upset and have the courtesy to leave me alone. But no, two older women approached me and stopped. They were wearing elegant outfits and fashionable shoes, and I assumed they were wealthy. I looked up with my tear-stained face, as one patted my shoulder saying, in a heavy New York accent, "I know just what you're going through, honey. The same thing happened to me once, many years ago. You'll feel better someday and realize he wasn't worth it."

I sat in stunned silence and must've had a strange look on my face. I had no words to reply. Finally, the two of them walked away with their arms linked, clucking and tsking. Those interfering, but caring, old biddies thought I'd been dumped by my boyfriend or husband. I would've busted out laughing, if I hadn't been so terribly, terribly sad.

Soon after that, a voice announced over the loud speakers that passengers could begin boarding, starting with the last rows. Good. I was glad I smoked, so I could hurry onto the plane and maybe have a little more privacy. After getting settled in my assigned seat, I finally calmed down a bit or maybe just got to the point where I had no more tears to shed, at least for a moment. I pulled the complimentary magazine out of the pouch in front of me that also held the laminated pamphlet of safety instructions and the ever popular vomit bag, unused, thank goodness. I absentmindedly flipped through the magazine, stopping to glance at a photo or an ad that caught my eye, and then put it back. I turned and searched on both sides of my seat for my safety belt, clicked it into place, leaned back, and let out a huge sigh. I kept my eyes closed during take-off and tried to nap, but sleep was something my mind wouldn't allow.

I was exhausted, yet I couldn't sleep. There were too many unanswered questions and too many that had never been asked, except for the one-word-question: Why? It was the question uttered hundreds of times, receiving no answer. Why did this happen to my sister? Why her? Why not someone else? Why not a bad person somewhere? I could feel a headache beginning over my right eye. That's where the worst ones always began. Every now and then, I'd be lucky, and it would only be a sinus headache, but usually it would become a full-blown migraine and knock me for a loop. That's when I began to panic. What if I got such a bad migraine, right here on the plane, that I threw up? What if I couldn't make it to the restroom? Or would I have to actually use the vomit bag? Don't even think that. Just put those thoughts out of your head, and you'll be fine.

I reached into the magazine pocket again and yanked the magazine back out. Just get your mind on something else, and you'll be okay. I began to flip through the pages again, only with more gusto and flapping of paper. I was determined to get through this flight without falling apart. Suddenly, a few words caught my eye: "One night, I dreamed I was walking along the beach with the Lord." It was an advertisement to purchase a plaque of the poem, "Footprints in the Sand." As I kept reading, it felt like a prayer, especially the final sentence: "The years when you have seen only one set of footprints, my child, is when I carried you."

What an impact! I believed I was meant to read those lines at that particular moment. It had such a calming effect on me and I made it home to St. Louis without any breakdowns, headaches, or nausea. (Ron met me at the airport and consoled me as I continued crying all through the terminal. We'd only been married about a year and a half and I was so grateful to have him in my life.) I would turn to those comforting words so often during the coming months and years, but they alone weren't enough. I didn't achieve a sense of ultimate healing until sometime later.

My Sister, My Mother, My Friend

The death of the extraordinary singer, musician, and entertainer Ray Charles in 2004 triggered me to delve deeper into myself and finally attempt to put into writing my feelings about my sister Jo Ann who'd been deceased for 20 years.

She'd been a huge fan of Ray Charles; and when I was growing up, I was forced to endure many hours of his records on our hi-fi, especially on Saturdays, housecleaning day. We'd listen to an entire stack of albums, while we swept and mopped floors, dusted furniture, and scrubbed bathrooms. Because she and my brother, Mike, really liked his music and because I could be an obnoxious teenager sometimes (Don't believe that one bit!), I'd complain about being forced to listen. I much rather hear my favorite MoTown groups or The Beatles.

Over the years, though, I learned the error of my ways and began to love his songs, plus lots of other standards. It's such a benefit belonging to a family of various ages. I was introduced to many styles of music. When I was five years old, I sang "Purple People Eater" all around the house and a couple of years later, "Itsy Bitsy Teenie Weenie Yellow Polka Dot Bikini." I loved those funny songs, but I also liked The Harmonicats, Chet Atkins, and Glenn Miller records my mother and dad played. There are so many songs that, to this day, can either bring a smile to my lips or a sadness in my heart. Memories begin to wash through me, and I'm transported back in time.

In 1983 shortly after Jo Ann's 46th birthday, she was diagnosed with a brain tumor. One of the hardest parts to accept was the fact that she'd been seeing all kinds of doctors, and none of them could figure out what was wrong. She had debilitating headaches, dizziness, and double vision, which finally forced her to use a walker! She lived near Miami, Florida, which was full of specialists for every disease from A to Z. Why didn't one of them discover what was wrong? Why didn't one of them see the cancer in the X-rays? Why? Why? Finally, doctors performed surgery but couldn't save her life.

They said if they removed too much of the cancerous brain, she might live but would be a vegetable. Jo Ann was given six months to a year, and she lived ten months. I called her as often as I could afford, sent lots of cards and letters, and flew there to visit her twice. The first time was when she had the surgery, and the second time was just days before she died.

Those were the hardest months I've ever been through. She was there in Florida, and I lived in the St. Louis area. There was no way I could afford to leave my job for any period of time to be with her. I had regrets about that for years; but in those days, there was no way Ron and I could survive without both our incomes.

She made the decision years earlier that she didn't want a funeral, and her husband honored her wishes, donating her body to science. There was no service of any kind, and the rest of us just kind of went back to our "normal" lives. I was so devastated by her death; it was then I realized that funerals aren't needed for the deceased, but they are so important for the ones still living. I needed that closure, that ritual, that time to mourn. And since there was no service, I pretty much completely fell apart.

After a couple of months of barely being able to make it through a day at work without constantly crying, I turned to a therapist for help. I'll never forget sitting in her warm and welcoming office with its comfy furniture and lovely plants. It also contained several boxes of tissues strategically placed throughout the room. I talked about the relationship I had with Jo Ann over the years, and she said, "My God, you've lost your mother!"

Right then, it clicked. I understood my sorrow and depression because she wasn't just my big sister, but also my friend and my mother in so many ways. Even though I loved my mother, my bond with Jo Ann was different and more complex. I was 30 years old when she died and I'd recently begun to feel like her equal. We had so many wonderful and fun times together, especially after I left John when I was 25, and lived back in the States. She'd call and we'd talk on the phone, we wrote letters to each other, and she'd either come to St. Louis for vacation, or pay for Scott and me to visit her. It's funny how age differences narrow as we get older.

During Jo Ann's final days, I had fantasies of trying to contact Ray Charles and ask him to please go see my sister. I would explain to him what a big fan of his she was, how she had all of his albums, plus a few 45s. I'd tell him how much it would mean to her (and to all of us) if he could go to Miami to talk to her. I never actually tried, and some days I wish I would've had the guts to do so.

Even now, almost 30 years later, there's hardly a day that goes by that I don't think about her, if only for a fleeting moment, and the memories are always happy ones. When I play my Ray Charles CDs, I sing along just as she did. I get up and dance when I can't sit still, exactly as she did. And if I'm driving my car, I do my wiggle-butt dance, as she did, too. I truly believe she is smiling on me every time I do that. And who knows? Maybe she finally met Mr. Ray Charles after all.

The Short and the Annoying

Every single day, no matter if he was sitting at his desk or scampering through the halls, he whistled. Although we had Muzak piped in, he whistled. He never veered to whatever song played overhead. It didn't seem to matter to him—even if one or more of us hummed along to the songs drifting out from the speakers. No, he seemed to like only one song. Day after day. All.The.Time. The theme from the 1954 movie, *The High and the Mighty.*

His name was Ralph, and he and I shared a large office space for a couple of years with two other women. He was a funny, little man and the first adult male I ever met who was as short as, or shorter than me—five-foot-nothing. He barely sat still for more than a minute. He fidgeted. He bit his fingernails. He was super hyperactive before it was ever discovered, defined, or diagnosed.

His desk was diagonally across the room from mine, kind of facing me. Although I wasn't aware of it for the first couple of weeks, there was a cylinder air tube mechanism in the wall behind his desk resembling the ones in bank drive-thrus. It sent and received shipping orders and other paperwork out to the warehouse and back.

Like I said, he was very fidgety, and I didn't see anything behind him. So every time that container came crashing down, I thought it was him jumping out of or falling out of his chair. Even when I jerked my head up to see what the loud clatter was, he'd already be standing, up and off on another caper to go see somebody about something—and revving up those first few notes of his one and only favorite song.

He could've been the poster child for ADD/ADHD at the age of "54 and a half." What adult ever adds "and a half" to their age? That's how Ralph was: childlike, honest to a T, and always wanting to please—always trying to help. That was his catch phrase, "I'm just trying to be helpful. I'm just trying to be helpful." Never uttered just once—always repeated in speedy delivery. He worked with three women, plus a woman supervisor. We were all younger than Ralph, and he drove us nuts. Our supervisor was a thirty-two year old woman, whose sanity hung by a thread on most days.

"Ralph, just go sit down. I'm handling this, okay?"

"Okay, Charlotte. I was just going to run these few orders over to the electrical department, though, and have someone sign off on them."

"Thanks, Ralph, but like I said, I have it under control. And that's why we have these inner office mail folders, too. I'll send it over, and it will be taken care of."

"Okay, Charlotte. I'm just trying to be helpful. I'm just trying to be helpful."

I'd have to say I've always loved hearing *The High and the Mighty*, but I didn't want to listen to it every single day, and especially just the first few notes, over and over and over. In the movie, John Wayne whistled the beautiful, haunting melody, and nobody, especially Flyweight Ralph, comes anywhere near Heavyweight Duke.

Rocky Loses by a TKO

Right after Ron and I got married, we inherited a puppy. There I was, 30 years old, and getting my first pet! Well, when I was a little girl we had goldfish a few times, but that doesn't count. Who wants a pet that you can't cuddle and play with? Oh, and there was that time my brother, Mike and I received pastel colored baby chicks at Easter. Not a happy outcome…..

The puppy was small, newly weaned, cute, fluffy and huggable. His soft fur was mostly black, with tiny patches of light brown above each eye and on all four legs. We weren't sure of the puppy's breed, but it didn't matter at the moment. My then 11-year-old son, Scott, named our new pup. He chose "Rocky" and the moment he bestowed it upon our newest family member, it fit perfectly.

Over the next few months, Rocky grew bigger by the day, the hour, the minute. At six months old, his paws were almost as big as the palm of my hand. That's when we learned Rocky was part Gordon Setter and part some-kind-of-a-really-big dog.

You know how intelligent adults sometimes do the stupidest things? At the time, we lived in a small.

two-bedroom apartment on the second floor of an old complex. Ron and I both worked full-time and Scott obviously went to school. Still, we thought leaving Rocky home alone all those hours during the day was perfectly okay. After all, he was paper-trained. But we soon learned he was not house-trained.

Our beloved puppy became bored, so he searched for things in the apartment to amuse himself with. Rocky's antics became so common-place that I knew every weekday—at 3:15, when Scott got home from school—my office phone would ring, and Scott would recite Rocky's activities for the day. I didn't even say hello anymore. This daily phone call became the highlight of the afternoon for my co-workers.

"What did he do today?" I'd sigh to Scott. The men and women in my office would stop what they were doing. A hush of silence filled the room as they leaned my way and sat perfectly still. It was like those old E.F. Hutton commercials.

As I listened to Scott's account, my facial expressions would change from shock or surprise to disbelief or anger. On some days I just gasped and snorted:

"He did what?"
"Oh my gosh!"
"Are you kidding me?"
"Can you clean it up?"
"Did you tell him 'bad dog'?"
"Well, close the cabinets."
"Well, close your closet."
"Well, shut the drawers."

I'd then hang up and fill in the details for my eager colleagues.

Rocky's days were always filled with mischief. He had a fondness for standard dog provisions— shoes, newspapers, magazines, tennis balls—pretty much anything he could find in the apartment. He even teethed on my lovely Bentwood rocker. I wondered and worried how he could eat the things he did and not get sick. He chewed up and evidently swallowed chunks of our dilapidated couch, including foam stuffing, fabric and wood. And one day, he managed to dig out our wedding album and chomp on some of the photos, leaving visible bite marks.

In a way, I was surprised our downstairs' neighbors never complained of noise, but I assumed they worked during the day, too. Then one morning, I received the dreaded phone call. It was from my elderly apartment manager.

"Hello, Becky?" I immediately recognized her raspy, smoker's voice.

"Mildred! What's wrong?"

"I think you better come home. There's been a lot of racket going on in your apartment, and some people have complained." She coughed and hacked for a while before continuing, "I walked over that way and heard it before I got to your building. Your dog was barking like crazy and it sounded like things were falling and breaking inside."

"Oh, my gosh. I'll get there as soon as I can."

I slammed the phone down, grabbed my purse and dashed out of the office. "I gotta go. Rocky's in trouble," I hollered to my co-workers.

I barely remember driving home or pulling into the apartment building's parking lot. I was too preoccupied with images floating around in my mind. *What could possibly have happened?* I thought to myself. I ran into our building and dashed up the flight of stairs. It was absolutely quiet when I reached our door, which I hadn't expected. I hesitated, then silently slid my key into the lock and slowly turned it, afraid of what I would see.

As I swung open the door, I immediately saw Rocky sprawled on the floor, apparently exhausted from the morning's events. Scattered all around him were pieces of my once beautiful, massive philodendron, missing so many leaves it resembled a vine. Most of the tiny nails which served as a trellis in the wall were also gone. *I hope he didn't eat them, too,* I worried.

I quietly stepped inside the apartment and surveyed the damage. Tip-toeing between little mounds of dirt, stems and leaves, I knew my cherished plant would never be the same again. The situation was so terrible that it was actually funny, and I couldn't help from laughing. That's when Rocky looked up at me with his tired, sad eyes. He didn't even lift his head.

I'm sure he's humiliated. I bent down and patted him. I then whispered soothing words. "Poor baby, Rocky. What happened here today? Did that bad old plant attack you?"

I smiled and he began to wag his tail, slapping it against the hardwood floor. That's when he stood up and I noticed that dirt was also in his fur. It was in his ears. It was in his nostrils. He began to shake from head to tail and dirt flew in every direction. As he walked over to his water bowl, I bent down to dig through the layers of soil and found some nails. I was fairly certain he hadn't actually swallowed any, but if he did, it wasn't many and I was sure he'd be okay. We always said he had the stomach of a goat—nothing made that dog sick.

I should've expected something like this to happen. Often when Rocky loped past that plant, the sheer movement caused the leaves to flutter and wave. He seemed a bit skittish and occasionally growled at it.

It was only a matter of time that the two would battle. Pound for pound, that big lug outweighed his opponent by 50 pounds. But the philodendron had the secret element—the element of surprise. Poor Rocky never knew what hit him. I'd say he lost by a TKO, and there was plenty of evidence to prove it.

Men Ought to Be
a Four-Letter Word

When I was in my forties, I had a hysterectomy and my doctor said to stay in bed for a couple of days and especially don't go up and down stairs. Our bedroom was on the second floor, so Ron did everything for me those first two days. He brought food and drinks, a book or magazine, anything I asked for. I didn't want to bother him much, so I didn't ask for much. I really didn't!

I was working for his company at the time and didn't want to get too far behind, so I did some paperwork while propped up in bed. At least I could attempt to keep up with that part until I was back at my computer.

Now let me just say that Ron is ordinarily a really great guy, a kind and considerate husband; but on the evening of Day Two, he wasn't being his ordinary self at all. In fact, he was being quite the opposite. Doing what little laundry and cooking there was, plus "waiting on me" was making him crabby.

I wanted to change into a particular pair of pajamas that night. They were the softest, most comfortable pair I owned, so I hollered as loud as I could, "Honey! Do you know where my pink jammies are?"

"What?"

"I said, 'Do you know where my pink jammies are?'"

Silence. Then thump, thump, thump. His footsteps got louder as he approached our bedroom. Standing in the doorway, he said, "What were you saying? I couldn't understand you."

Oh really? You couldn't understand me? Maybe it was more like you couldn't HEAR me, since you have the TV BLARING!

"I said, I'd like to put on my pink pajamas, but I don't know where they are. I think you washed them in a load of clothes. I even got up and looked in my dresser, but they're not there."

I assumed they were wadded up in a basketful of clean clothes, next to the dryer, which just happened to be downstairs in the basement. And I knew how much he hated going up and down stairs. He then gave me one of those looks and said, "Do you really *have* to have those particular ones? Can't you wear something else?"

That did it. I hadn't been a bit demanding and my feelings were hurt, plus I was pissed. The words just burst out of me. "You know what, Ron? Men ought to be a four-letter word!"

Oh my gosh. I'm a genius. I didn't even notice his reaction because I was already daydreaming, envisioning a sales plan: Mass marketing of bumper stickers and t-shirts and baseball caps spelling it out for the world to see: Men Ought to be a Four-

Letter Word --MENN. I could see the dollar signs and hear the cha-ching of cash registers as my bank account overflowed with money. There were so many instances where millions of women would want to say those exact words.

She: "Honey, would you vacuum the family room for me?"

He: "I don't know how to use the vacuum."

She: "Menn!"

~ ~ ~

She: "Darling, could you unload the dishwasher for me?"

He: "I don't know where all the dishes go."

She: "Menn!"

~ ~ ~

She: "Sweetheart, would you mind removing all your stuff that's piling up on the dining room table?"

He: "I don't know what to do with all that junk."

She: As she thinks of telling him what he can do with it, says: "Menn!"

~ ~ ~

How about it ladies? I'll do the marketing if you'll do the purchasing!

MENN

A Joyous Journey

As I slowly made the turn into our driveway, I saw that the garage door was open, and there stood my husband of four years. It was a cold, windy day in March of 1987, and he was wearing a hat. That's about all I remember. I'm sure he must have had on a coat or jacket, but all I remember is that knitted cap. I rolled to a stop, put my car in park, pulled the emergency brake, and just sat there for a moment while his eyes met mine. He looked at me with an inquisitive look and raised his eyebrows, as if to say, "Well? What did you find out?"

I picked up the book from the passenger seat that the doctor had given me during my appointment. I held it up to the windshield with the title side facing him. His expression changed from curious to disbelief to shock in the two or three seconds it took me to begin crying—again. The name of that book was *Pregnant and Lovin' It.*

We had not planned on having a child of our own. We both had been married once before. He had two sons: a 20 year old, and a 16 year old, and I had my son, Scott, age 14. For one thing, we thought we were too old! We were dealing with teenage boys and trying to "semi" blend our sons into a family. (And as I've professed many times since then, "Real life **ain't** like *The Brady Bunch*!")

But as it happened, it seemed there was another plan for our lives that we weren't aware of at the time.

Some things were happening to me or not happening as it were, so I made an appointment with my gynecologist. On March 30, 1987, the doctor uttered in his charming British accent those now infamous words, "My dear, you're pregnant!"

What? How can this be? How did this happen? All those ridiculous, rhetorical questions kept repeating themselves in my head. I was still deep in thought when I sat in our driveway, gazing at Ron. I don't believe I will ever forget that image of him. It was as if the outline of the garage was a stage, and he was part of a play.

It only took me 24 hours to arrive at the final emotions: joy and happiness! I was thrilled with the idea that I was going to have another baby! Did I want another boy? I loved little boys! Or did I want a little girl, since our family was already full of boys? It didn't matter, as long as the baby was healthy.

After my emotional roller coaster ride, it was April 1st before I started telephoning family and long-distance friends and began the conversation with these words, "This is *not* an April Fool's joke. I am pregnant!"

Those months of pregnancy were some of the happiest of my life. I hadn't felt so healthy and full of energy in a long time, and I ate everything in sight! Even though the technology was already available to detect the baby's sex before it was born, Ron and I decided to be old-fashioned and wait to be surprised.

On October 20, 1987, Mark was born by a scheduled C-section. Another boy! We were thrilled! Ron was able to be in the operating room with me, and I was so happy that he was able to share this miracle with me. But the nurses whisked Mark away, (Oh no. It's déjà vu, just like when Scott was born. What could be wrong?) Soon we were told that our baby had some fluid in his lungs and wasn't breathing properly. He was kept in a special area of the nursery, with tubes attached in various places. It was heartbreaking, not being able to pick him up and cuddle him. Ron and I would walk down the hallway to see him and touch his little fingers and toes, and caress his little face, but we weren't allowed to hold him or give him a bottle.

I begged my doctor to let me stay in the hospital until Mark was well enough to come home. But insurance companies have their rules. I was forced, for lack of a better word, to leave the hospital without my newborn son.

After arriving home, all I could do was gaze at Mark's new crib and his tiny clothes. I said about a million prayers, asking for a miracle, if that's what it was going to take to bring him home.

Astonishingly, he began to improve immediately, and we were told we could take him home on October 26, which was only two days after my release. Joy set in, but also fear. What if he really wasn't ready to be released from the hospital? What if he needed the expert care that he could only get there? The nurses assured both Ron and me that our baby was fine and ready to go home with his adoring, devoted, and doting parents! Bringing him home was one of the happiest days of our lives. We would jokingly argue over whose turn it was to give him his bottle, even those middle of the night feedings. We both loved him so intensely.

We raised him with love and compassion. We demonstrated our spiritual faith and also displayed our faith in him. We always expressed our belief that he could accomplish anything he truly wanted in life. Through all these years he has made us very proud parents.

Live Your Dream

When well-meaning friends and relatives heard that Mark had applied to only one college, the statements were generally like these:

"Shouldn't he apply to at least one other college, just in case?"

"What's he going to do next year if he doesn't get accepted?"

"I know he's smart, but look at the odds."

Even though my husband Ron and I had some of those same thoughts, we never wavered in defending his decision and supporting him all the way. After discussing the situation at great length with him, we knew no other college would do. It was Washington University in St. Louis or *nothing!*

Mark had always been an intelligent student, and college was hopefully in his future. Sometime during high school, he heard it was the best university in the area for mathematics, and math was his passion at that time. He liked reading math books the way most people enjoy reading fiction. I would pick up one of his books, flip through it, and see numbers and symbols that only looked like Greek to me. (I found out later, a lot of them were.)

Ron and I joked about where Mark might have acquired such a mathematical brain. I claimed it was from *my* side of the family! My deceased father had once been a math teacher at a small college and later became an aeronautical engineer. The "math gene" seemed to follow only the males in my family because I understood only the simplest equations and barely passed Algebra I in high school. My brother Mike was quite good at it, and tried numerous times to help me with my homework until he finally threw up his hands in exasperation.

In July of 2005, the summer between Mark's junior and senior year in high school, he e-mailed David Wright, chair of the math department at Wash U. He introduced himself and asked if the professor could possibly speak with him, either in person or by phone, for help and advice in his pursuit for advanced math knowledge. Professor Wright promptly replied and invited Mark to visit him the next week.

The day of the visit, Mark collected some notes he'd written, and brought a pencil and note pad. I went along, too because I wanted to meet Professor Wright and let him know that Ron and I were behind Mark one hundred percent.

What transpired that day will stay with me for the rest of my life. I watched and listened as Mark spoke in math terms I'd never heard before. The entire situation mesmerized me, especially when Mark stood at the blackboard and wrote out a huge equation he'd been working on. It covered the entire board, and reminded me of the scene in the movie *Good Will Hunting*. It was truly a surreal moment.

Professor Wright was impressed with Mark's calculations and amazed with his desire and ability to work them out. He was kind and gracious and immediately put him at ease. After their discussions, he browsed through his bookshelves with great consideration and suggested some titles and authors for Mark to read.

As we left his office and walked down the beautiful halls of such a distinguished place of learning, I know neither Mark's feet nor mine ever touched the floor. I looked up at my handsome son who towered a foot over me. He appeared to be in the same state of pride and happiness as I was. We talked excitedly about the events that just occurred, each wanting to make sure the other heard the same praise and compliments. My son's dream seemed as if it just might be within reach after all.

Throughout the rest of his school year, he was idealistically confident about his acceptance. Ron and I were the ones worrying, knowing how devastated he would be if he did not get in.

During those months of waiting, I came across a quote by Henry David Thoreau, which became one of my favorites: *"Go confidently in the direction of your dreams! Live the life you've imagined."*

We received the exciting news on March 17, 2006, two months before Mark graduated with honors from high school. He indeed had been accepted to the one and only university he wanted to attend. The acceptance letter also stated an amazing fact: There were 22,000 applications for a class of 1,350. Some dreams do come true, especially if you work hard and walk in the direction of those dreams.

~~~

Mark graduated from Washington University in 2010 with a bachelor's degree in philosophy. He is now a graduate student there.

Through the Years

Whenever I'm seated in a restaurant, I enjoy glancing around the different nooks and crannies, watching various couples sitting at the tables and in the booths. I like to speculate about which ones are on a date with someone new or which ones are dining out with their usual partner. Being within hearing range isn't even important. All that is necessary is being able to see their facial expressions.

As a young teenager, I promised myself I would never become one-half of the married couple that just sits and stares off into space.

Oh my gosh. I would think to myself. *How can they have nothing to talk about? Are they that bored, unhappy, or miserable? Have they stayed in a loveless marriage, for whatever reasons?*

I will never be like that! I would announce to myself, only in the silence of my mind. I knew I would never fall out of love with **my** Knight in Shining Armor, whoever he may be.

I find it strange that I actually believed that, considering all the hurt I endured because of my parents' divorce.

Ah, the naivety of youth! Those self-promises about love and marriage go hand-in-hand with the ones about what kind of mother I would be. *I* would never yell at my child in the checkout line at the grocery store. *I* would never allow my child to have a pacifier. *I* would be the perfect model of patience, love, and understanding!

Even though my life hasn't turned out the way my teenage self-envisioned it, I really did find a prince of a man—the second time around. In spite of recent divorce statistics, and especially those for second marriages, mine has been a glorious success. My husband Ron and I celebrated our 30th anniversary in February 2013.

How did we accomplish such a feat, you may ask? If I was forced to provide a one-word answer, I'd have to say: *Love*. But that, of course, is such a cliché. The reasons are as different as they are numbered. We both have a great sense of humor. We come from the same religious backgrounds, which I believe is extremely important. We were blessed with the birth of our son. We both shared the same viewpoints on child rearing and overcame the obstacles that accompany a relationship involving stepchildren, as in step-teenage sons, as in what I wrote in a previous chapter: Real Life is *not* like The Brady Bunch! In short, we both were willing to work hard to make our marriage last.

Of course, we've had our arguments. In the past, we argued about the same things most couples do. We've tried to follow the rule of never going to sleep angry, but we even failed a time or two on that. The longer we've been married, the shorter the list has become of things to disagree about. Funny how that seems to work. With age, and a little wisdom, we've realized so many things just aren't worth arguing about, and that we don't always have to be right...especially me!

Ron and I have always loved to make each other laugh. He has more of a dry wit, and I tend to just be goofy. I love "breaking into song," usually when he least expects it. I might use my opera voice, or my Patsy Cline voice, or anything in between. I also do crazy dances around the house to which Ron will say, "Be careful, Bea. You're gonna hurt yourself." (He's always called me Bea.)

During the height of "Brangelina Fever," while we both were acting particularly goofy in the kitchen one evening, Ron turned to me and said, "Do you think Brad Pitt and Angelina Jolie act like this?"

We both responded with the exact same words: "I doubt it!"

I'm not trying to paint a picture of a completely blissful life, either. Of course, there have been times I went through bouts of worry, anger, and sadness, but Ron was there for me. For years, I tried to establish a father-daughter relationship with my estranged dad, but it never became what I truly wanted. Ron was always there, listening when I needed him to, and saying the words I needed to hear. During our second year of marriage when Jo Ann died, he was there again, listening, comforting, and holding me, while I shed so many tears.

And I do things for him, small things like making his favorite chocolate chip fudge cake with double fudge frosting, or by traveling for hours and hours in a car because he refuses to fly.

We care about each other's feelings. We have the "give and take" that is obviously essential in a happy relationship. And since I only have one life on this earth, I'm eternally grateful that when dining out with my wonderful husband, I've never, ever stared off into space.

How Things Change....in 29 Years of Marriage

"Ahhh, this is the life!"

Becky and Ron -- 1983

"Ahhh, this is the life!"

Becky and Ron 2012

* My very talented friend, artist Stephanie Piro, drew this 2-panel cartoon for my blog in 2012, as Ron and I celebrated our 29th wedding anniversary. I described the kind of scenes I'd like and she brilliantly came up with the drawings! Thank you again, Stephanie!

The Answer Was Right in Front of Me

It never did work properly—that new dishwasher of mine.

When Ron and I bought our second house in 2003, we brought along our refrigerator from our previous home, kept the stove that came with the new house, but decided to buy a new dishwasher. We went with a brand name we knew and trusted, chose a middle-priced model, and felt we had made a "good choice."

I don't remember exactly how soon I realized our "good choice" wasn't working up to par, but I was unhappy with it almost immediately. I should have complained to the store we bought it from, taken it back, and asked for a replacement. Why I didn't do any of those things, I can't really say. I guess I thought it was too much of a hassle, especially with everything else involved in moving, and it was just easier to keep the darned thing. Was it possible I wasn't using it correctly? I don't think so. I'd read the directions, more than once, and I was certain I knew how to follow simple instructions.

As the months and years went by, my complaining became a nightly ritual as utensils came out with gunk stuck to them, pots and pans weren't clean, and plates would still have remnants from the evening meal. I experimented with different detergents and wash cycles, tried residue and spot removers, but still hand-washed many items, after they came out supposedly clean.

I lightheartedly began to blame it for my messy, cluttered kitchen, saying it was giving off bad karma. Then the disorder spread throughout the house, as other rooms became more and more disorganized. It was definitely turning into something much larger than a faulty appliance; it was becoming an emotional feud. I began to imagine yanking it out from under the counter top, with an evil glint in my eyes, and whacking it to bits with a sledgehammer.

I simply could not justify getting rid of it though, since it still cleaned *some* items. So, I began to intensely wish and hope it would just completely break down, and then I would finally have a legitimate excuse to buy a new one. The thought of not having a dishwasher in the 21st century wasn't even a consideration. Until, that is, it actually sputtered its last gasp of steam and shut itself off. I decided I didn't *want* one, at least not yet anyway. I told my husband, Ron, that I would just continue washing everything by hand until we could get the more expensive one I really wanted. Imagine his surprise and bewilderment when I informed him of my new plan.

"Are you sure you don't want a new one? That's all you've been ranting about for months!"

I cheerfully responded with, "Yes honey, I know! Isn't it weird? But I honestly want to do this, just like I did for so many years when we didn't have a dishwasher."

He gave me one of his *looks* and said, "Whatever you want. But I think you're going to regret it, especially when we have friends or family over, and there's a ton of dirty dishes."

I mulled that over and knew it was obviously a possibility, but I wasn't concerned about that at the moment. I was just looking forward to doing my dishes the old-fashioned way, with suds, a dishcloth, and some elbow grease! What in the world had come over me? It wasn't merely the matter of money, even though that was a factor—it went deeper than that. Part of it was due to my nostalgic outlook on life. Even though I felt as if I couldn't possibly live without gadgets such as my laptop and cell phone, part of me yearned for those simpler times, those younger days, those years without dishwashers. I wanted that again: the time to linger, to think, to just *be*.

With my kitchen window positioned right over the sink, I could look outside while I washed and rinsed, using that big, empty dishwasher as my drain rack. Since it was summertime, I had such lovely things to watch: birds flying to and from the bird feeder out in the back yard or squirrels and rabbits nibbling at the fallen seeds that landed in the grass. There were always the comical antics of a squirrel scampering up the pole, hanging on the feeder upside down, and getting his fill until a large blue jay would swoop in and chase him away. I really didn't mind if he shared the birdseed, but I always laughed when he jumped down, scurried away, only to come sneaking back another time. Actually it could've been a different squirrel, couldn't it?!

I've always loved looking at trees, too, the way they stand motionless during calm days or wave lazily in the gentle breezes. The best part of all, though, was the new wind chimes I'd recently purchased and hung right outside that kitchen window. How glorious their sounds! How mesmerizing and lovely to watch as the pipes gently swayed and tapped each other. Even when the wind picked up and they clinked and clanged, it was still a beautiful noise.

Although simple pleasures are all around us, sometimes it takes something like a broken-down appliance or heavenly sounding wind chimes to make us actually be aware of them. Now my time spent in the kitchen is always enjoyable, whether I'm cooking, baking, cleaning up, or just plain gazing out the window. I am so grateful for all the appliances I have and especially for that one I don't have!

~~~

This chapter was written long before 2013, the year we moved into our townhouse.

Self-Centered Sadie

My sister Marian and I flew into Des Moines several years ago for a short Iowa vacation. As usual whenever we arrived in the evening, we stayed overnight at Sadie's, a distant relative by marriage. She always invited us, especially since she lived practically next door to the airport. It was already late when we got there, and the three of us went out to get a bite to eat. Marian and I were both exhausted and looked forward to a good night's sleep.

Sadie was a widow and had been married to our mother's first cousin, Charles, who passed away many years ago. She was so excited about our visit that she followed our every step, talking nonstop the entire time. She even followed us into the guest bedroom as we tried to hint at how beat we were. Finally, as it became apparent that our huge, lioness yawns weren't getting the message across, we began to unpack our pajamas. We managed to get in a couple of words, such as: "really tired" and "need to go to bed" and "need to get some sleep." Still, her nonstop talking continued. So, we did what any grown females would do in such a situation. We undressed right in front of her, slipped on our

211

jammies, and crawled under the covers. As her side of the conversation continued, ours ended abruptly when we both fell sound asleep.

Over the years since that visit, we've talked and laughed about that night many times. We don't think Sadie ever realized how funny the situation was, at least to us.

I've bestowed upon her the name "Self-Centered Sadie" because she accumulated several antiques over the years, which as a rule is perfectly acceptable, but a couple of them didn't even belong to her. They were left to Marian and me from our maternal grandmother and/or great aunt. Mine was a beautiful, ornate bowl, and Marian's was a glass compote dish. Somehow, Sadie acquired them first and did not want to part with them, at least not yet. My God, the woman was in her nineties, my sister was in her sixties, and I was in my fifties! What was she waiting for? Sadie would most likely outlive both of us, and we'd never be able to enjoy them. This was a situation we did not find funny, as in the falling asleep episode. We thought it was rude and insensitive of her to hang onto things that weren't even hers in the first place. During various times over the years, whether Marian and I were there together or on separate visits, we always asked very politely if we could please take our bowls home "this time," and the answer was always, "Oh, no. I'm not ready to give them up. And besides, I've got everything written down as to who gets what when I'm gone."

Yeah, like that would work out well for us, since we lived hundreds of miles away. She never had any children, and it was up to a couple of her nieces to get the items to the correct people. Our cousin Nancy also asked on our behalf when she visited Sadie, but the answer was always, "No, not yet."

I doubt if those antiques were even valuable, money-wise. That wasn't the point. The point was that she wouldn't let us have what our blood relatives wanted us to have, which meant a great deal to us.

The last time I visited her, I went in with a Game Plan. I was determined I wasn't going to leave her house *without both items*. I stayed an appropriate length of time, chit-chatting about this and that. Her physical health had deteriorated somewhat. She used a walker to get around even in her small family room. Her mental capacity was still perfect, though, so I then decided it was now or never. I tactfully asked for the two bowls. She hesitated for a second, and I jumped right on it. I explained how I would wrap them up carefully and take such wonderful care of them—how Marian and I had both waited so long to have them. She again hesitated but shuffled along toward her basement door, and that's when I hopped up from the couch. I knew our treasures were stored down there. She opened the door and took a couple of slow steps, while I followed close behind. Although she hadn't actually said she was going to give them to me, I assumed that was about to happen. *This is it! I'm finally going to get them this time! I can't believe it. Marian will be so happy!*

She then mumbled something about just taking a look at them, like every other time I'd been there, as if they were museum pieces. That's when I spoke the words I was sure would persuade her.

"You know, Sadie, Marian turned 70 this year. Don't you think she should have her compote now, so she has some time to use it?"

"Really? 70? Oh, how time flies. Well....how is her health?"

"Oh, she's in great health!"

"Well, good then. She'll live a lot longer and can wait awhile to get it."

Un-freaking-believable! I couldn't believe she just said that. She caught me off-guard. Why didn't I think to say Marian was in very poor health—near her death bed, even. Geez.

Well, I did manage to talk her out of *my* bowl that day, but I honestly don't remember what I said. She wouldn't give me the compote, though. She claimed she still used it, in a whiny, little girl voice.

As soon as I could, I got the heck out of there before she could change her mind about my bowl. I felt so bad for Marian. She resigned herself to the fact that she would most likely never get the compote dish that was intended to be hers.

~~~

Sadie passed away a couple of years ago, sometime after I began writing this chapter. I'm sorry to say Marian never did receive her compote dish, but she didn't waste any energy being upset

214

about it. I don't know if I would've handled it so maturely, had it been me.

From Pigtails to Chin Hairs

Cell Phones Can Be Dangerous

Some of the craziest things are always happening to me. I share some of them in other chapters: falling down steps, tripping over things, riding my bike into a concrete ditch, and the pièce de résistance —the crowbar incident.

But this next little episode was more of a Twilight Zoney kind of happening.

I can't really remember what month it was or even what season, for that matter. Ron likes to keep our house really cool in the summer. We're talking cold, walk-in freezer kind of cool. So, it's not unusual for me to wear a hooded sweatshirt around the house in the middle of July. And it could've even been winter, because we keep our house fairly cool then, as well.

I'm telling you all that, so I can tell you this. One afternoon, while wearing a hooded sweatshirt, I decided it was time to listen to the phone messages on our answering machine. My cell phone was in the middle pocket of my sweatshirt, and I didn't think a thing about it. As I leaned against the kitchen counter, listening and starting to jot down names and numbers, I thought I heard a teeny, distant voice saying, "Hello? Hello?" I listened a little longer and heard it again. I couldn't figure out where the heck it was coming from. I knew neither the TV nor radio was on. The windows and doors were all closed. Finally, I realized the miniscule voice was coming from my stomach! Well, not really my stomach. It was coming from my cell phone, which was in the middle pocket, right next to my stomach.

I grabbed my cell phone and looked at it. Somehow, as I leaned against the counter, it had dialed my cousin Nancy, in Greenfield, Iowa! She, in turn, answered her phone and was hearing far-off, tiny voices herself, the ones which were coming from my answering machine!

I immediately hit disconnect because I sure didn't want Nancy to hear any of my messages, such as Macy's, telling me my payment was late. I called her right back, though, told her what happened, and we both laughed ourselves silly.

Yes, indeed, cell phones can be dangerous—especially when they start making calls without your knowledge.

Out of the Mouths of Babes

Several years ago, Ron and I began celebrating various holidays with our grown kids and grandkids on the weekend before the holiday. It became a necessity since we have a blended family, and the other parents and in-laws involved, needed their times, too. We made the decision partly for ourselves, but most of all for our kids, so they wouldn't feel torn in their loyalties, and they could actually enjoy the day.

A few Christmases ago, I thought it would be fun for all the grandkids to stand in a circle around our large and much-loved dog, Tiger, while everyone, including Tiger, sang "Jingle Bells." As we all stood and sang with gusto (except for the little one on his mother's lap), Tiger howled like a hound dog. The joy all the kids felt was obvious by their smiles and laughter.

A couple of months later, on Ron's birthday, we were babysitting our then, seven-year-old grandson. When the three of us gathered around the kitchen table to light the candles on Ron's cake, I asked if he'd like Tiger to sing "Happy Birthday" with us. Right away, he thought that was a terrific idea.

I turned off the kitchen lights, lit just a few candles to signify the occasion, and again, Tiger howled along with us. We could barely keep singing because of our grandson's delight and giggles. Right after we finished the song, we allowed him to help blow out the candles, and he asked in all seriousness, "How many other songs does Tiger know?"

~ ~ ~

Another year, Ron and I stopped to see some of our grandkiddos early one October 31 so they could show us their Halloween costumes before they went out trick-or-treating.

One of the youngest boys gave me lots of attention and hugs, which was unusual for him. I of course accepted with glee, and gave hugs back to him in return. As I leaned down toward his cute crew cut hair, I inhaled a lovely smelling shampoo.

I told him how wonderful his hair smelled and asked what kind of shampoo did his mom use on it? Since he was a little guy, I couldn't quite understand him the first time, and I thought he said, "Cake shampoo!"

So, I teased him a little and said, "Cake shampoo? Your mom uses cake shampoo on your hair?" And he just fell over giggling.

I said, "Oh, it's not called that? Please tell me again what you said."

Still giggling, he managed to look back up at me and said, "Pink shampoo!"

"Oh, pink shampoo," I said, as I laughed along with him.

Cake, pink—they both sounded a lot alike, especially coming from his angelic, little mouth.

Would You Like Potato Chips With That?

In January 2010, I traveled to an amazing conference in West Des Moines, Iowa—a combination writer's workshop and spiritual retreat, which truly was a life-changing experience. I went more for the writing aspect, but discovered the most powerful was the spiritual.

I found the event while searching online for winter writer seminars. (Who in their right mind looks for winter-writing-seminars, and doesn't go somewhere warm?) I knew from the description it sounded like something I'd definitely like to attend. The name of the location was Hamilton's, and there were lovely photos of various fireplaces throughout the meeting rooms. Luxurious chairs and couches to recline on, plenty of space to just meditate, and a reasonably priced hotel located right next door.

The seminar was, "Writing from the Soul" and presented by two fantastic women: Joyce Rupp, who is a Servite Sister (nun), author, teacher, and speaker; and Mary Kay Shanley, also an author, teacher, and speaker. The two of them transformed thirty totally different, unique women in those few short hours from strangers to kindred spirits, becoming connected in a way that will never end. The majority of the women were from the Des Moines area, and some of them already knew each other. There were a few who came quite a distance: two or three women from New York and New Jersey, one from Wisconsin, and then there was me. I came from Missouri. What a fabulous group we had: different ages, religions, and backgrounds. Some were there more for the spiritual part, some for the writing. I can honestly say I was there for both. I sincerely felt ready for more spirituality in my life, and of course, I'm always searching for "writerly" wisdom.

Although I'm used to cold weather, it was bitterly cold that January, and I was thankful all I had to do was bundle up and walk back and forth from the hotel to Hamilton's. I think the temperatures were 15 degrees for the high and minus 5 degrees for the low.

The event began on a Friday evening at 6:30 pm and ended at noon the following Sunday. Sometime during her presentation that first night, Joyce (she doesn't go by "Sister") spoke of when she taught at a school many, many years ago in downtown East St. Louis, Illinois. You know those Cosmic-Karma-kind-of moments? You hear or see something that is such a coincidence, a happenstance, a fluke, that you *know* you were meant to be there? That's what happened to me when I heard "East St. Louis."

Later that evening, I talked to Joyce and found out it wasn't the same school, but it ignited a spark within me that burned all through the seminar and for weeks afterward.

Whenever I entered or left the building, I used the back door because it was the handiest to get to the hotel. It was at the end of a long hallway, and right before walking out into the cold, I passed a small gift shop that always seemed to be closed. The door was partially glass, so I peered in, and I could see a couple of racks of greeting cards, hanging wind chimes, and small statues. Hmm, it looked like *my* kind of gift shop—kind of a miniature Hallmark store. I'd have to remember to ask when it might be open.

The next day, I didn't have to ask because when I was blown into the hall by a huge gust of bitterly cold wind, I saw the door was partly open. I pulled off my stocking cap and gloves, unwound my wooly scarf, and knocked on the door.

"Hello? Anyone in there?"

Nobody answered, so I went inside a little farther. I decided if I left the door wide open, it would be okay to browse just a minute. It would be obvious I wasn't trying to steal anything. Once I actually walked inside and saw the cards and gifts, I realized exactly where this spiritual/writing retreat was taking place: a funeral home. Hamilton's was a mortuary!

The cards were sympathy cards; the gifts were for the grieving—and in an area toward the back of the store just a few feet from the door and almost in plain sight, a selection of caskets. I was surprised to say the least. I hadn't seen any indications what kind of building this was. I went through a variety of emotions, mostly surprise and then amusement. *Hmm, no wonder there's a feeling of life changing, spiritual happenings in here.*

During our get-togethers, we listened, learned, shared some of our innermost thoughts, shed a few tears, and also laughed with glee. We were constantly provided with wonderful snacks and drinks: coffee, hot tea, hot chocolate, water, and soda (or as they say in Iowa "pop"!), Plates of cookies, brownies, snack cakes, fruits, dips, peanuts, and pretzels. At lunch on Saturday, we were served delicious box lunches and dinner the last night was a scrumptious catered buffet. Food for our souls and our bodies!

The beautiful, authentic fireplaces added warmth, joy, comfort, and camaraderie to the setting. There were moments when we sang and danced in the areas near them, and the flames danced right along with us. One I particularly loved was *The Elm Dance.* Our instructor explained that Joanna Macy took the dance with her to workshops she was leading in areas poisoned by the Chernobyl nuclear disaster. The city of Novozybkov was the most occupied and contaminated, and the dance became an expression of their will to live. It was there the dance evolved a distinctive form with the raising and swaying of arms, evoking their connection with the trees they so loved. It was an amazing experience I will never forget.

During our box lunch, a distinguished looking gentleman wearing a dark green apron meandered around the room, appearing to be part of a catering company. He had extras of the individual bags of chips and asked if anyone would like another bag or two. As he weaved around, he pleasantly made small talk with everyone, whether handing out snacks or cleaning tables. When introductions were made at the table next to mine, he was the last to speak and said, "Hello. It's nice to meet all of you. My name is [so-and-so], and I'm the embalmer."

Gulp.

I looked at the three other women at my table and the look on their faces was priceless, and I'm sure I looked a little weird myself. As in more weird than usual. Getting up quietly from our chairs, we wadded up our empty wrappers, and skedaddled out of that room like school girls running out of the cafeteria after making a scene.

Women, girlfriends, writers, laughter, prayers, songs, poetry, tears, and never ending memories. To say the weekend was a life changing experience is an understatement. I wasn't ready to leave when it was time to go, and I wondered if that's how some of the deceased "felt" when it was their time to exit and pass through the magical doors of Hamilton's.

I Was Born with Klutz Genes

A Bike, a Prop Plane, and a Trench

Are some of us just born a klutz? Are we the unfortunate ones who inherited a "klutz gene" in the thousands of genes in our bodies? I believe it's true. There's no way a person could do the idiotic things I do or have the bizarre accidents I have, without it being part of my DNA. Thank you very much, dear ancestors. It's bothered me for quite some time, wondering what the heck is wrong with me. I know I haven't had a lifelong inner ear problem or anything. And it's not as if I'm top heavy, which might cause me to tip over without a reason. Clumsy, I am, and you'd think I'd be used to it by now and pay more attention to my actions and my whereabouts. Uh, nope.

I break fingernails by somehow stabbing my nail into the tiniest crevice in the door hinge of the clothes dryer, and by bashing my knuckles into the oscillator of the washing machine while pulling out the damp laundry. I've had the pleasure of receiving numerous bumps and bruises from knocking into furniture that has been in the exact same place for years.

The majority of my painful accidents always involve my clumsy feats. I mean feet. Well, and my vision, too. The one that stands out the most happened when I was about 12 years old. I was riding my bike home after school one fall afternoon and appreciating all the gorgeous colors of the leaves. The streets on my route were neighborhood ones, so I didn't have to worry about traffic and getting run over, at least not that day.

As I've mentioned, I've always been enchanted with airplanes, especially the sight of prop planes. There is just something about them that thrills me; I'm not sure what, really, and it's probably a combination of things: their unique engine sound, the fact that they remind me of days gone by, the propeller itself. And of course, they always make me think of my dad.

That particular day, I heard one flying over and immediately glanced up, trying to quickly find it while still pedaling. I was on a street that I remember having the name of Boul, and there was something unique about it. A trench/gutter/drain sort of thing ran the length of it, about three feet deep, made of brick and/or concrete. I don't remember ever seeing any water in it, though. I was riding on the right side of the street, and it was on the left. As I kept watching the plane putter along, I obviously didn't pay attention to where I was going because the next thing I knew, I'd ridden/fallen right down into that gutter thingy. I've often wondered why I didn't get terribly hurt, or my bike wasn't damaged. I bumped my face on something—maybe the handle bars or the front basket—but that was my only injury. It was just a little scratch that left a tiny scar over my right eye. I can't believe I didn't lose a tooth (or teeth!) or break any bones or poke an eye out.

It took me a minute or two to realize what had happened, and then I immediately whispered a quick prayer of thanks. After that, embarrassment set in, and I looked frantically around, hoping no one had witnessed my incredible stupidity. It didn't appear so. *Whew.*

The hardest part was getting back out of that darn gutter. Being a little weakling trying to push my bike up the incline was almost impossible. And I had my books and purse in the basket, too. Somehow I got out of there by myself and simply pushed my bike the rest of the way home.

I know I told Mother, Mike, and Jo Ann about it that evening, but I can't remember what any of them said. I guess they didn't realize what a big deal it was and how I could've landed in the hospital or something. Too bad there wasn't *America's Funniest Videos* back then. I'm sure I would've won if someone had taped it.

Somersaults and Stairways

This is the kind of thing that happens to me all the time. Some are more painful than funny, and some are way more funny than painful. Take for example, my staircase somersault. It happened one night when Mark was in high school. A few of his

229

friends stopped by. I was upstairs and I went to answer the door. The hallway and staircase were all dark, but I thought I had walked down all the steps and made it to the foyer. Wrong! I missed the last step, and I immediately did a perfect 10.0 somersault directly onto the hardwood floor. I then stood up and answered the door, greeting the boys with a smile and hello without missing a beat, as if nothing strange had just happened. As I recall, they said they thought they heard a thud, but didn't see anything through the glass pane in the front door.

~another example years later~

It was morning, and I was in the kitchen making coffee. Ron was upstairs getting ready for work and hollered down asking for a particular shirt of his from the laundry room. He, thinking he's being nice and helpful, stood next to the upstairs banister and said, "Don't come all the way up. Just toss it up, and I'll catch it." Okay, that's fine. We've done this hundreds of times. I'm not the best tosser-upper, but it usually works after a couple of tries. This time, I go up to the third step, thinking I'll be able to throw it high enough from there.

"Good job, Bea! (Have I mentioned that Ron calls me "Bea"?)

"No problemo, honey."

Why I didn't turn around to walk down the steps, I have no freakin' idea. I stepped back one step, then another, thinking my foot was going to be on the floor. Wrong. I stumbled and fell flat on my back on the hardwood kitchen floor, my head just missing hitting a corner wall that stuck out. I lay there for a couple of seconds, realized what had happened, and started half-crying and half-laughing. My tailbone hurt and the back of my head hurt. I couldn't believe Ron didn't hear all the commotion, especially the big thud when I hit the floor. I started yelling for him.

"Ronnnn! Come and help me! I've fallen off the steps and I can't get up!"

Finally, he walked over to the upstairs landing while he talked on his cell phone. I was still moaning and groaning, as he talked away to a customer.

Uh, hello! I'm kind of hurt down here!

Then he said, "Oh, my wife just fell. I have to hang up."

Ya think?

He came down the steps, leaned over, looking at me and said, "Bea, what happened? Are you okay?"

"I fell down the *$#&% stairs again!"

He helped me stand up and inspected my head for any bumps, bruises, scratches, or blood. We both went on with our morning routines; while I wondered when the time would come that I'd ultimately fall and break into pieces.

A Football Game and a Flying Pretzel

In 2006 Ron and I went to a football game at Washington University in St. Louis. The stadium is small with bleachers only on one side of the field. Home team fans sit on one end of it; the Away team

231

fans on the other. Ron and I attended because we were excited about Mark being admitted to Wash U, and we wanted to support the college in any way we could. Besides, we like football.

We paid our couple of dollars to get in and then got programs and drinks. We chose seats close to one end, about two thirds of the way up. After sitting there for a little while, we realized we were in the Away seats and certainly didn't want to make that faux pas. Since we were already close to the top, we decided to walk behind the sports booth and down the other side. I'm naturally a fast walker, so I was way ahead of Ron. I glanced back once, and he was coming along fine. The next thing I knew, I was stepping over some kind of metal pipes that were screwed into the cement. I looked back to warn Ron to watch where he was going, so he wouldn't fall. Instead, he was just standing there, gawking at the buildings and trees as if they were something momentous. I hollered, but he couldn't hear me; and the next thing I knew, I was on my hands and knees, palms scraped and burning, while soda, ice, and a warm pretzel went flying through the air. The force of my fall caused a slight lack of bladder control, the final humiliation. And here's the real kicker . . . Ron didn't even witness my fall! He was still staring at the scenery.

I looked back at him, hoping for some help and sympathy, but it was too little and too late.

"Bea, what happened? How did you end up on the concrete? Did you fall? Are you okay?"

Don't open your mouth yet, Bea. Count to 10 or 100. It's not his fault. Oh, yes it is.

"I was looking back and hollering to tell you to watch your step, so you wouldn't trip and fall on one of these stupid pipes. But nooooo, you were too busy checking out **leaves** and **bricks**. So, *I* fell instead."

"Oh, I'm sorry you fell, but it really wasn't my fault, ya know."

I was boiling mad inside. My palms were starting to sting. My soda was gone, and my jeans were damp. We made our way over a couple more pipes and down some steps. We easily found some empty seats and sat down. I became a little less aggravated at Ron because, of course, I knew it wasn't his fault. I was just so mad at myself for once again being a clumsy klutz that I wanted to blame someone else. I couldn't blame Washington University for having those dumb things on the cement walkway, could I? Not on your life. So, as usual, the more I thought about it, the funnier it became.

I knew for a fact at least one person saw me fall. A man had come out of nowhere and looked startled as I crash-landed. God, I wondered if anyone else had seen me. Thank goodness it hadn't happened in *front* of the bleachers. I would've been ten times more humiliated. Most of my acrobatic spectacles happened indoors and at home, so this one would've been a real show-stopper.

The more I thought about it, the more I laughed. The more Ron and I talked about it, the harder I laughed. Falling and laughing – two things I have a real talent for.

Hanging on to Vern, Unsuccessfully

With all my falls and klutziness, I've still managed to live through my thirties, forties, and fifties, without any serious injuries. It didn't take very long to find out what I might do to myself in my sixties, either. Just two months after my 60th birthday, I took such a loud tumble that even though I fell on carpet, the witnesses couldn't believe I didn't get hurt. Yes, that time I had onlookers which only added to my embarrassment.

It happened on a Thursday evening, when a man and his six year old daughter stopped by to look at some furniture we were selling. Ron and I were finally going forward with our plan to downsize and had begun getting rid of items we knew we wouldn't need and/or have room for.

While we talked in the family room, our beloved dog Vern, who had been out in the back yard, decided he wanted to come in. It was bitterly cold, and he *really* wanted to come back in. Whenever we have company, Ron usually takes care of hanging onto Vern's collar until he gets over his initial excitement. But that night, for some reason, I thought I'd be able to handle him. Big mistake.

Vern lunged and pulled me for a few seconds until I couldn't hold on any longer. As I let go, I flopped onto the carpet just as Ron jumped up and grabbed Vern. Most of my weight landed on my left knee, left elbow, and left cheek bone. My glasses flew off my face and I was more worried about them being broken than any of my bones. Surprisingly, nothing was broken. My glasses were okay and all I wound up with were a few painful bruises. It took me a while to get up off the floor, and during that time, I heard Ron asking if I was okay. By then he was standing over me and sounding very concerned. I also heard our potential furniture buyer asking about me, too. After I got up, I said to him, "Oh, I fall all the time. I'm just a klutz but I never get hurt."

You know how when you think later about something that definitely wasn't funny, but you start to laugh uncontrollably anyway? That's what I did that night after I got into bed. I tried reading for a while but all I could do was think about how hilarious I must've looked. Besides the fact that I fell, I suddenly disappeared from everyone's view because I fell directly behind our love seat. One minute I was bent over, hanging onto a dog's collar and the next....Poof! I was gone with a thud.

I Tumbled Down the Hill with a Barbecue Grill

There's a creek and woodsy area behind our new townhouse where Vern goes to do his business. Ron and I share the duty, always use a leash, and regularly take doggie baggies for whatever gets "dropped." Vern and I have a certain routine of walking up and down a small slope as he moseys along the driveway. We've done it zillions of times and he always knows when and how to back up and out of an area. (Do dogs generally know how to back up? Our other two, Rocky and Tiger, never did.)

For some strange reason, a neighbor keeps his Weber Grill, with its big round lid, stationed precariously near the top of the small hill. We've adapted to its placement and usually stay clear of it with no problem. It's a wonder it remains in place since it has three legs, two of which are attached to a wheel. Normally, if he sniffs behind it too close, I gently pull on his leash, he backs right out and continues trotting along in front of it.

During a recent, early Sunday morning, Vern was particularly interested in something deep in the shrubs. He sniffed, pulled, and moved farther behind the grill, as I hung onto his leash. Instead of trying to back him out of there, as he's used to, I thought I'd let him continue on forward. So I decided to lead him frontwards, but while he was still on the back side of the grill. He got confused and turned the opposite way, so before I could lift the leash up high enough, he and I kind of "clothes-lined" the grill. As it began to roll down, I tried to stop it, and somehow slipped or tripped, bounced around a bit and fell down the little hill. As I realized I was going to land on the driveway, I just knew I was going to be knocked out or killed. I sure didn't see my life flashing before me. I only saw the concrete and knew this was going to be bad, really bad. I landed on my back, butt, and head on the hard concrete. As that was happening, the grill's lid fell off and clanked, my glasses and baseball cap flew off my head, and my cell phone slid out of my pocket.

I laid there for a few minutes and knew I hadn't broken any bones, thank goodness, but my left knee and left arm hurt quite a bit. I wondered if anyone heard or witnessed my noisy tumble, but I really didn't care one way or the other. I was so glad I had on jeans, because I could tell my left knee was scraped and bleeding, and it would've been a lot worse had I worn shorts. I managed to sit up, then stand up, and slowly picked up my scattered belongings. I also pushed the grill back up to its spot and replaced the lid.

Vern and I walked home. I cleaned up my scrapes, applied Band-Aids, and crawled back into bed. Ron wasn't a bit aware of it until a couple of hours later when he woke up and I told him all about my latest escapade.

"It's a miracle you haven't gotten seriously hurt, you know that?!"

Yes, I do. I sure do.

Ron Scares the Hell Out of Me!

For as long as I can remember, I've had a very low energy level. I inherited my dad's hypoglycemia, and sometimes it's hard to function. When I was in high school, I took naps. When I was a stay-at-home mom, whenever I could sneak one in, I took naps. When I worked full time, I'd come home almost every night and sleep on the couch before or right after supper. You get the picture. I wish with all my heart that I had tons of it, but I don't. So on those few and far between days that I do have a lot of get-up-and-go, I'm really happy because I get lots accomplished; and as a result, I feel really worthwhile. I had one of those days a few years ago…

I did some laundry, whipped up some homemade (from a box) brownies, picked up clutter around the house, worked on my homemade birthday cards, stopped at the library to pick up a book, stopped at the post office to mail a package and get some stamps, etc. I was still in high gear after my husband had gone upstairs to bed. I made several trips up and down the stairs, returning things to where they belonged. One of those times, as I walked up the steps, I carried an armful of folded t-shirts and was talking to our sweet dog, Tiger (who is now deceased), as she followed faithfully behind me. Assuming Ron was watching TV in the bedroom, I was in my own little world...that is until I reached the first landing and saw something out of the corner of my right eye. He was standing there, resting his elbows on the railing, just waiting for me to look up and see him. And when I did, he scared the absolute *%^#$ out of me! I was *so* mad at him (because he scares me all the time by appearing out of nowhere). Anyway, I was so mad, I think I danced in place for a second or two, screamed, threw the t-shirts at him, and cussed like a sailor! Besides being scared within an inch of my life, what makes me the angriest is that he always acts **so innocent**! He always says, "*What? What did I do? I was just_____!*"

Yeah, fill in the blank: "I was just standing there, walking into the room, waiting for you," and so on.

I would've loved to have seen the look on my face. Every time I've thought about it, I start cracking up, which aggravated me at first. But still, in afterthought, it *was* funny! It makes me think of the kitchen scene in *Ferris Bueller's Day Off*. Ron's lucky I didn't react the way Ferris's sister did when Mr. Rooney, the school principal, surprised her in the kitchen of the Bueller home. She screamed and quickly karate kicked him three times—right in his face. I think it's the funniest scene in the entire movie, and I love to watch it over and over again.

Ron, all I can say is, "Beware. You just may surprise me one too many times!

Why Do I Say These Things?

A few years ago, I worked part time at a major bookstore near my home. The atmosphere, the overall mood of both staff and customers, and the extra employee perks held me captive. Compelled to remain there, I stayed almost a year after my seasonal time ended. When the economy began its downward spiral, my hours were cut to where I spent far more than I earned. That's when I knew it was time to quit.

Being a writer and book lover, I still shop there as often as possible. There aren't many activities I'd rather do than browse among shelves of novels, memoirs, self-help books, cookbooks, dictionaries, maps of the world, and everything in-between.

When I heard Fannie Flagg had a new book out, that was all the incentive I needed for another visit. The title escaped me, but I knew one of the associates would look it up for me. As I walked toward the service desk, I recognized Jane, one of the employees. Although we'd never actually worked in the same department, I knew her fairly well. Her personality was the exact opposite of mine. She was quiet, reserved, and soft spoken. That day, she seemed particularly quiet, almost listless and indifferent. I assumed she was still engrossed in previous questions from customers or simply tired and overworked.

"Hi, Jane. I'm looking for that new Fannie Flagg book, but I can't remember the title."

She uttered a vague hello as her fingernails clicked away on the keyboard. While waiting, I took in all the activity around me. Customers of all ages strolled up and down aisles. For a moment, the thought crossed my mind to apply for a job again, but fortunately, it vanished as quickly as it had arrived. Never taking her eyes away from the computer screen, as if daydreaming, Jane said in a distant, detached way, "I still dream about you."

"You do? Wow! That's really cool. Sometimes I still dream about this place, too; and it's been a long time since I worked here."

I rattled on and on about how my goofy sense of humor must've really made an impression on her and how I hoped her dreams were funny ones. She didn't bother to interrupt me until after I'd basically made a complete fool of myself.

When she finally looked up and made eye contact with me, she said, "No, Becky," in her matter-of-fact tone. "That's the title of the book: *I Still Dream About You*."

For a split second, I was speechless. My mouth dropped open, and I could feel the heat creeping up my ears. I knew they were turning bright red. My eyes darted back and forth, as my mind fully grasped the ridiculous things I'd just said. Had anyone else heard me? Why didn't she just say that in the first place? All she had to do was add those three extra little words. Three. Little. Words. "The title is …"

Oh my god! Can you spell i-d-i-o-t? What made it even worse was that Jane didn't seem to realize how funny this was. She never even cracked a smile. She merely stepped away from the counter and walked ahead of me. As she meandered between various tables and book displays, I trotted along behind her, trying to keep up and blathering on and on about my embarrassment. I kept trying to explain my misunderstanding and how hilarious it would've been if she really had dreamed about some of my crazy antics at the store.

"No, I have other, more important things on my mind," Jane said almost gruffly. She stopped, picked up the hardcover, turned and handed it to me.

"Oh my gosh, yeah. Well, I'm sure you do! Well, then. Uh, okay. Bye!"

It seemed like we couldn't get away from each other fast enough. Or maybe it was just me. I practically galloped over to the café area, glanced back and watched her stroll away in the opposite direction. She had such good posture; I daydreamed she was a model, balancing a book on top of her head, and the title of it was *How to Handle Awkward Situations.*

From Pigtails to Chin Hairs

Kindness in Aisle Nine

A few years ago, I experienced two separate, thought-provoking incidents at two different grocery stores.

I'm naturally a people watcher; so I don't understand how some people just walk through life with their blinders on and not notice the daily lives going on around them. Particularly in the world of retail shopping, there are plenty of faces to observe. Some are happy; some are sad. Some look tired, some look angry, and some just look beaten down by life.

The first encounter happened as I stood in line with a couple of items in the express lane. As I waited, I looked all around and noticed an elderly woman hunched over her shopping cart, walking ever so slowly. I wondered why someone wasn't shopping with her, and I felt concerned. She stopped and must've asked one of the stock men where a certain item might be located. I couldn't hear what was being said, but I saw him turn, point, and refer to an aisle number on the opposite side of the store. He turned his back to her and continued stacking cans on the display end. She kept trudging along the way she was originally headed, most likely giving up on the idea of buying something she obviously wanted.

As I watched her, I wondered why the stock man had not offered to go and get the item for her, why no one else seemed to notice that she could use a little help, and if I should even interfere at all. How sad to be ignored, as if she didn't matter. I decided to approach her and ask if I could lend a hand. It certainly wouldn't take long, and I'd easily find another place in line. She smiled, her eyes lit up, and she graciously thanked me. She told me about some pickles she wanted that were on sale. I asked the pertinent questions (sliced, whole, dill, sweet, etc.) and walked down the six or so aisles to get two jars for her. I walked back, told her I hoped I had chosen the correct kind, which she said I did, and I asked if she needed any other help. She said no and thanked me profusely for my kindness.

As I returned to the checkout line, I noticed that nothing much had changed in my absence. The checker continued scanning customers' purchases, weighing the fresh produce to determine their prices, and stated the amount due without much, if any, eye contact between them. The bagger asked each and every shopper the magic question, "Paper or plastic?" Check books, debit cards, and car keys were swept off the counter sometimes accompanied with a mumbled, "Thank you." People hurried out the automatic doors and continued on with their day.

As I got into my car, I noticed a young man sitting in a handicap parking spot with his radio blasting. I wondered if he had driven the woman to the store and didn't even bother to go in and help her. I have no way of knowing for sure, but why would he be parked there? If he wasn't waiting for her, surely it was for someone else who might need assistance. Images of that experience drifted through my mind for a day or so, and then I nearly forgot about it—until a few days later.

I truly couldn't believe it when I saw the same woman in a different grocery store. This time, almost the same set of circumstances was happening, and I felt as if I was having some kind of vision. What was happening here? Was I having déjà vu? Was I being tested for some higher reason? Was she here at this very moment for my benefit?

I walked over to her, said hello, and asked if she remembered me and the jars of pickles. At first, she hesitated and then smiled. I asked if I could help her again, but this time she declined. She began to tell me, though, where she lived and that she'd like to live with her daughter. But her daughter was busy with her own life: taking care of her house and her children and working full time. Her daughter didn't want her, and wanted to put her in a "home" somewhere. She said she could understand how someone wouldn't want an old person living with them and disrupting their lives.

As I listened, I felt helpless, knowing there was nothing I could do. I gave a sympathetic pat on her arm and hinted that maybe she had misunderstood the situation.

I said goodbye, hoping she really wasn't as lonely as she seemed. As I walked away, I said a little prayer that she would always experience random acts of kindness no matter where she was, even in aisle nine.

They're Not Real Doctors, You Know

I grew up in a home where chiropractors were thought of as quacks. The word "chiropractor" itself was pronounced with such disdain that even as a little girl, I knew I didn't want to ever see one. I was even afraid of "real doctors," those with an M.D. after their names. My parents, though, considered them to be God-like. They faithfully followed all their instructions and advice, and they also trusted nurses, pharmacists, and dentists. But chiropractors? My mother practically shuddered at the very thought.

My parents' comments replayed in my mind throughout my teenage years and into adulthood. Chiropractors are quacks. They will not help. In fact, they might cause more pain and possible injury. Just stay in bed for a few days, and that will fix it.

In my early twenties, I realized nothing I tried "fixed it."

During those years, I picked up and held children, hauled laundry baskets, lugged bags of groceries, made beds, vacuumed—all those tasks that might potentially harm a person's back. By the time I reached my late thirties, I experienced various types of pain all too frequently. Some were constant dull aches; others were sharp and severe. Still, I didn't know what to do, which way to turn, or what doctor to see.

One day at work, bits and pieces of a co-worker's conversation floated into my office. Certain I heard the word "chiropractor," I sat quietly at my desk, commanding my phone not to ring. I eavesdropped further and heard, "Old Doc so-and-so. Really helped. Twenty bucks." Hmm, maybe I'll ask her for more information. Would having a referral drive away my deep-rooted fears? Maybe it was time to find out.

Never seeing a chiropractor before, I had no idea what to expect. My first visit to Old Doc's place seemed rather peculiar, though. He definitely was old—old enough to be retired— but obviously still seeing patients. His hair was snow white; he was medium height, slim, and wore a threadbare button-down shirt. He looked quite frail. *Oh great, he should really be able to help me.*

His practice occupied two small rooms in his equally small house. One was the waiting room. The other was the torture chamber. Fortunately, I didn't hear any screams coming from that room, so my apprehension lessened to some extent. When patients exited, they didn't appear hurt or traumatized either. Another good indication. When it was my turn, he called me into the exam room. He pointed at a stack of twenty dollar bills resting on his ancient, marred desk and a handwritten sign that read, "Cash Only."

"Place your money right there, Missy. Then show me where your back hurts."

I added my twenty to the pile and then moved both hands around to my back. I pointed to the area and said, "Down here, kind of at my waist line."

"Well, step on over here, stand on the ledge of this table, and we'll fix you right up."

Although he used the word "fix," I had no idea how he could possibly do that since the table was vertical. There appeared to be a hole for a face to fit in if I was over six feet tall, which I wasn't.

My co-worker had neglected to mention how eccentric Old Doc was. But being in so much pain, I didn't care. I just wanted to stop walking crooked and not hurt anymore. Taking as deep a breath as I could, I climbed up and stood there no matter how ridiculous it seemed.

Old Doc pressed a button and the table slowly went down until I was lying on my stomach, completely horizontal. Pretty neat contraption, especially if someone was unable to climb onto the adjustment table.

"Now, scoot yourself on up here, so your head fits in that hole. I'll have you all fixed up in no time." There was that word "fix" again.

The old guy's strength amazed me. He pushed and pressed. My back popped and cracked. I grunted and groaned. It took all of two minutes, if that. Then I magically began my ride back to an upright position. Stepping off the ledge, I hesitated and then thought, *Oh my gosh. He really did "fix" it.*

That was twenty years ago. When Old Doc passed away, I searched for a new chiropractor, knowing it wouldn't be easy. I tried a couple of doctors that were recommended by friends, but they just weren't the right "fixer" for me.

A few more years slipped by as I tried various exercises, over-the-counter painkillers, and ointments. Nothing helped for any length of time. Finally, a relative mentioned a chiropractor, and I felt encouraged again. From my first appointment, I knew Dr. Steve Schoenherr was the right *New Doc* for me. X-rays were taken of my back and neck, plus an in-depth consultation. He pointed out bone spurs on my spine, explained other matters in detail, and immediately won my trust.

That was six years ago and during this time, he's helped me in so many ways; suggesting simple exercises to do at home and also arch supports for my shoes. I haven't felt better in years.

Thank goodness I let go of my fears when I did. Sometimes it's so difficult to turn away from those beliefs we've been programmed with since childhood. Giving up should never be an option when trying to find answers for a healthier, essentially pain-free way of life. Mother and Dad are deceased, but I wonder what they'd think if they knew a chiropractor "fixed" my back.

Keep Those Tweezers Handy

About five years ago, I discovered I had a chin hair. Not just a peach fuzz kind of chin hair. Oh no. It was a big, black, disgusting chin hair that only a vile, ugly witch would be proud to display.

A good friend I hadn't seen in many years met me for lunch at our neighborhood Bread Company. We had a wonderful time; enjoyed great food, and caught up on each other's lives. Afterwards, we sat outside in my car for a few more minutes. We just didn't want our perfect afternoon to end; but as our conversation slowed, she mentioned it and pointed to my chin. Yeah, outside in that bright sunshine, it was quite noticeable. I looked in the rearview mirror and almost had a panic attack when I saw it. Oh my god! Eeek! I inspected it for some time and couldn't understand why I hadn't noticed it. Thank goodness she told me, because I would hate for anyone to see it, family or strangers.

From that day on, I've consistently remembered to check for that chin hair. I'd pluck it when it was just a silly millimeter long. Until recently, that is. For the past few days, I kept feeling something tickly under my chin or on my neck. I assumed it was a loose hair from my head or a dog hair or other random fuzzy of no consequence. I swatted at it occasionally, until yesterday, when it finally began to drive me nuts. Exasperated, I stumbled into our half bath, yanked off my glasses, leaned forward, and peered into the bathroom mirror. That's when I saw IT—a huge, dark chin hair that was so long, it formed a large letter "C." Aaaackkkkk!

How many of my friends saw it and didn't bother to tell me? How many people had seen that disgusting thing? Shoppers in stores, probably shaking their heads, thinking: *That poor woman has the longest, ugliest chin hair I've seen since witches in movies.*

I grabbed my tweezers and yanked that thing out as fast as I could. I laid it on the vanity top and it immediately curled back into a "C" again. When I pulled it out straight, it was a full inch long. How do I know? I got my ruler and measured it! I should've kept it, framed it under a magnifying glass, and hung it in my bathroom as a reminder to perform a chin-hair-check often!

Thoughts on Love & Forgiveness

In May of 2001, I received one of those dreaded phone calls no one wants to receive. My brother Mike called to tell me our dad was seriously ill and not expected to live. I was quite surprised by my feelings, because Dad and I didn't exactly have the ideal father-daughter relationship. In fact, we hadn't really kept in touch for years. That was due to various reasons, mostly the fact that he divorced Mother when I was 10 years old. He lived in another state and didn't seem to have much time for my brother and me. There were missed graduations, forgotten birthdays, and promises never kept.

I particularly remember getting an idea in my head the Christmas I was 12 years old. I truly believed he was going to "*come to his senses*" and come home to us. (I'm pretty sure that idea came from my mother.) I sat for hours in our living room, facing the front door, listening to Bing Crosby croon "I'll Be Home for Christmas." I played that record so many times, I almost wore it out. I just knew any minute he would burst through the door, ask for forgiveness, and be loaded down with gifts for all of us, including Mother. It was a scene I played repeatedly in my wistful daydreams. I made sure the porch light was on, so Dad could find our house. But of course, that never happened.

Even after becoming an adult, I still held onto some deep-seated sadness. I guess the little girl's pain inside me would never completely go away. Yet I realized divorce is never just one person's fault, and I began to feel differently about Dad. I wanted to have him in my life again.

I'll never forget watching a movie on TV in the 1980s titled *Max Dugan Returns.* It was about a grown woman's dad returning to her life after years of separation, bringing outrageously expensive gifts and trying to make up for everything. That film had such a profound effect on me. It was so much like those young girl daydreams I'd had.

I wrote to my dad shortly after seeing it, and it was the beginning of a slow road back to getting to know each other again. Our letters, phone calls, and occasional visits were rare, and usually only initiated by me, consisting of uncomfortable attempts at conversation.

As the years went by, I told myself I'd forgiven him for everything, but I realized that wasn't true. That only happened after going to Iowa and seeing him in the ICU, knowing he was close to death. As he lay in the hospital bed, I held his hand and marveled at the softness of his skin. His hand was not the firm, muscular one I remembered seeing and grasping as a young girl. I felt tears roll down my cheeks as the emotions welled up inside me. I began to feel a love for him I hadn't allowed myself to feel in so many years. It was at that point I thought to myself that no matter what … he still *is* and always *will be* my dad. I began to pray for his recovery, and I asked God to give Dad and me more time together. He was 76 years old, and I barely knew him. I wasn't finished with him yet!

As he began to recover, I realized I could laugh at his know-it-all ways and excuse his flirting with the young nurses. He had been married *four* times, yet here he was a lonely, old man without anyone.

After he was released from the hospital, we talked on the phone and e-mailed fairly often. He told me things that amazed me concerning those years he was away. He said he truly didn't know the hurt he had caused us. He was so consumed with his own wants and desires, he really didn't understand the heartbreaking effect of his selfishness. Being a woman who cannot comprehend a parent leaving her children, it was very hard for me to understand why he chose to live his life the way he did; but that new found forgiveness let me know I didn't *have* to understand it. I simply accepted it. I decided I wouldn't let the past stop me from trying to be the daughter my dad wanted and needed. I wished he didn't live so far away because I wanted to help take care of him, but it just wasn't possible. Dad died the following year, a few days after Thanksgiving. I was saddened by his death but extremely thankful we had emotionally reconnected again.

Divorce affects so many people; and unfortunately parents can be so wrapped up in their own emotions, they don't realize what their children are going through. During the early 1960s, divorce was rare, especially in our Catholic community. My mother was so hurt, angry, resentful, and embarrassed, she scattered her emotions over and through our lives until my brother and I were as miserable as she was.

Mother died years before Dad did, so she never knew I came to terms with everything. I forgave her, too, for her self-pity during all those years and for her lack of desire to even try to find joy in everyday life. I never expressed those feelings to her, though, because she really wouldn't have understood.

A wise friend once told me she believes part of our journey here on earth is to forgive our parents. It took me a long time to forgive both of mine for not being perfect—for not being whom and what I thought they should be. As soon as I did, though, I felt the burden of anger, sorrow, and regret lift up and out of me. I was finally set free.

Precious Cargo

I hope you don't mind, but I brought my dad along with me.

I giggled to myself as I thought of the reaction my cousin might have if I actually uttered those words to her. Even though Nancy has a fabulous sense of humor, I couldn't bring myself to tell her, especially knowing her dislike of my father.

Nancy's house was the second stop on my Iowa vacation. She and her husband, Denny, always had the welcome mat out and the porch light on when it came to visitors. I was traveling alone this trip and had just completed a week's stay at my brother and sister-in-law's home in northern Iowa. We'd had a wonderful time doing those usual vacation things: shopping, eating, and reminiscing. They did, however, ask one very unexpected, completely astonishing question of me. They wanted to know if I would like to have *dad's ashes!*

"Huh? I didn't know dad was cremated! Why didn't anyone tell me?"

All I knew was that he donated his body to science, and there was no funeral or visitation. Those of us who cared, arranged to have a small ceremony on his behalf. That was *six* years ago.

"I guess we thought we told you. We really don't want to keep them any longer. Would you take them with you?"

I thought for a few seconds, trying to let everything I'd just heard sink in, and then said, "Sure. I'll take them."

After the initial shock, the next thing was as funny as finding out about the ashes in the first place. My sister-in-law opened their coat closet and pulled out a heavy cardboard box with a UPS label on it, still sealed. They had never even opened it! They had stored old Dad in the back of the coat closet, next to the vacuum cleaner and snow boots, never even looking inside.

We carefully set the box inside a large, brown paper bag, and I immediately thought of various places Dad might want his ashes spread. I'd have plenty of time to make a decision, so I wasn't in any hurry. Besides, he'd already spent a few years stored in a closet.

Days later, I walked into Nancy and Denny's house, carrying Dad along with me. I so wanted to say those words that kept running through my head, but hauling around someone's ashes may not seem so hilarious to some people. The shopping bag's contents remained a secret during my visit, stored next to my suitcase, laptop, and purse.

I then carried Dad back home with me—a place he hadn't been in many, many years.

~ ~ ~

It's been four years since I wrote that part of this chapter and not much has changed. I did take the box out of the grocery bag and opened the UPS carton, which held a taped box, and inside that, another one. I hoped it wasn't going to be like those Russian dolls that are stacked inside each other until there's just a teeny-tiny one left. But that wasn't the case. The last package held the one containing Dad's ashes. A small, gold plaque was on the top with an engraving of his name and some designated letters and numbers. I felt strange gazing at the information, knowing this was all that was left of my father— reduced to a name and number. It was kind of like when he came into this world with a name on a numbered birth certificate.

My first attempt to lift the keepsake box almost resulted in a couple of broken fingernails. I knew a person's ashes were heavy, but I had never tried grabbing a container of them before, either.

It looked wooden, but I realized it was heavy-duty plastic with a wood grain appearance. At first that upset me, but it was sealed shut, and I decided it didn't really matter what it was made of as long as the ashes were safely stored.

For quite a while, the bag remained in plain sight in our guest bedroom. What better place? Whenever Ron walked past the open door and noticed it, he'd shudder a little and make a remark of some kind.

I'd laugh at him and ask, "Why does that disturb you so much?"

"It gives me the creeps! I don't know why you aren't bothered by it."

"Heck, I don't have any hang ups about it. I like having Dad nearby!"

Relatives came to visit a couple of years later and stayed in the guest room. I knew the polite thing to do was to move the bag somewhere else before they arrived. As in the case when I stayed at Nancy's house, good manners were in order. I picked up the shopping bag by its handles, and that's when it began inhabiting the walk-in closet in our master bedroom. Again, it was in plain sight. *Hmmm, I wonder how long it will be before Ron notices it's in here now.*

Obviously, I saw the bag daily and sometimes more than once, but usually forgot about it the minute I walked away. At times, I paused and wondered what I should do. I knew what I *wanted* to do with those ashes, but I wasn't sure if it was legal or not. Plus, there was that little problem of actually getting the box open.

One day, I managed to get it onto the floor of our closet and sit cross-legged next to it, holding my handy-dandy flathead screwdriver. I'd succeeded in yanking open many an item using that particular tool, and I anxiously wanted to get a look at the ashes.

I poked and pried here and there, using both hands and all my might, but the seal didn't budge. It then occurred to me that *duh, these boxes were not meant to be opened.* They were most likely airtight, waterproof, and vacuum packed. Even if I was able to unseal it, I visualized that goofy waitress Vera in the TV show *Mel's Diner.* In the opening sequence, she is shown ripping open a package of straws that fly everywhere. *That* was exactly what I did *not* want to happen, especially in our clothes closet. Can you imagine it? A powdery substance exploding all over every piece of clothing, shoes, and purses in there? Only it wouldn't be just any kind of dust—it would be my dad's ashes!

Because of my joyous childhood days in Cahokia, Illinois, I so wanted to scatter some of them in the now empty grounds that housed Parks (Aeronautical) College back then. The few years my dad taught there were the happiest of my life. I've driven around the perimeter a few times lately, and it always breaks my heart. The remaining buildings have long been empty and stand dilapidated. Grass and weeds grow uncontrollably, even through jagged cracks in the runway; an obvious sign no one is around except people like me, and the ghosts of our memories.

From Pigtails to Chin Hairs

Prop Planes & Daddy's Girl

I wrote a version of the following poem, "Daddy's Girl," in early February 2012. Originally, it was meant to be prose but as I typed, the words felt more like poetry. It was one of those rare and special moments when the words just flowed, and that doesn't happen very often.

The weather was magically warm, and I walked in wondrous thoughts and visions. That's when it began to sink in. The cosmic, overwhelming sense that *then* was the time to get serious about my writing. It was the time to continue on with my memoir. Jump over those hurdles standing before me, and burst through anything or anyone (including myself) who got in my way.

Since that profound February day, I've seen and/or heard prop planes almost *every single day.* And the most Cosmic, Twilight-Zoney thing about it was when and where I see them:

- When Vern and I were doing our daily walk (at various times of day)
- When I just walked out onto our deck with my pen and tablet in hand

- When I was driving, and all of a sudden one would be flying over my car
- When I walked out to our mailbox
- When Ron and I would be sitting on our deck, just talking and resting
- When I was in a parking lot, walking into or out of a grocery store

The point is—there was no particular time of day or night!

~ ~ ~

It became such a regular occurrence all through that spring and summer, it made me smile and laugh every time. I'd look up at the plane, and then farther on up into the heavens and say out loud: "I see it. I see it! I'm getting it! Thanks! I'm getting it!"

Several times when I looked up, I swear the plane tilted a little and I'd say, "I see you, Daddy. Yes, I'm writing. I'm writing my memoir! Thank you!"

Daddy's Girl

I strolled along the pavement
the sound of quiet surrounding me
like a quilt. The stillness was deafening
until I heard the engine of a prop plane
flying overhead. Pausing and shading my eyes
I squint and watch it putter across
the powder blue sky.
Memories flood my soul
immediately tugging my mouth
into a wide grin.

The next day I walk the
same path. A distant cardinal chirps
most likely believing it's already spring.
And why shouldn't he?
These past few days have been nothing
but glorious.
Only the calendar page declares
it's just early February.
I turn, searching for his brilliant crimson color
among the vast bare branches
but my eyes cannot find him.

I notice the sky is full of vapor trails.
Those wispy, cloud-like streaks also
carry memories for the child within me.
I think back. All those years ago.
The newness of jet airplanes and the
thundering explosions of sonic booms.
My dad explaining the magic & mystery.

I close my eyes and for a moment
I'm standing motionless in my front yard again.
I stare up, marveling at the sight above
taking it all in and thinking as profoundly as
a five-year-old possibly can.

Blinking, I hesitate for a moment and
then become aware of
my present surroundings.
I begin my journey
back home.

Tomorrow. Maybe tomorrow,
I'll return to the same path,
thinking back and
reminiscing once more.
Sentimental journeys.
Always bittersweet.

Becky and Tara at Habitat for Humanity of St. Charles County (Missouri)

Annual Celebration of Trees Gala 2010

Part VI:

Miscellaneous

From Pigtails to Chin Hairs

Tara's Story

<u>Note</u>: This next chapter is the result of my meeting a sweet and soft-spoken woman, Tara Rhodes, at the first HFHSCC (Habitat for Humanity St. Charles County) *Divas Building Dreams* breakfast meeting in May of 2009. The keynote speaker was Brenda Warner, wife of Kurt Warner, former quarterback for the NFL St. Louis Rams. I also had the privilege of being introduced to Brenda who was sincere and unpretentious.

~ ~ ~

"It takes hands to build a house, but only hearts can build a home." ~ Author Unknown

Tara Rhodes's life changed dramatically on August 29, 2005: the day Hurricane Katrina blustered into her life and the lives of countless others. The magnitude of the storm's fury left a physical aftermath of warlike destruction and an emotional impact that would never completely fade away.

Before that ill-fated day, Tara's life was similar to that of many women. She was a single, working mom with two young children and considered herself happy, in spite of struggling moneywise. She never really considered moving because she liked the climate, even though her soul kept feeling a persistent tug that God did not want her to be in Mississippi.

Two weeks after the hurricane, Tara was finally allowed to go back into her neighborhood and inspect her townhouse. What used to be her home was a shambles. She discovered one bright corner, though, which kept her from falling completely apart. Her "praying closet" was partially intact. That was the name she had given the walk-in closet in her bedroom. It was her private, little haven where she kept a chair, her bible, and other essential documents. As she trudged toward it, she was utterly shocked to see that one side of the closet and its contents were soaked and damaged, but the side that contained those important papers and her chair, was dry, including her bible, still open and ready to provide words of comfort. Bible verses did console her for a while; but as time went by, she also couldn't help but ask the questions: "Why me, Lord? Why did this happen to me?"

During the next few months, Tara and her two children, Michael and Terrika, shuffled from place to place, which eventually brought them back home to Missouri. Although Tara believed she had already experienced her lowest possible state of mind, that didn't occur until the day she and her children walked into a homeless shelter in downtown St. Louis. She felt so humiliated and out of place as she observed the destitute and unkempt people surrounding her— many who suffered from mental or substance abuse. *We don't belong here*, she thought to herself. As she waited for her number to be called, she held her children closer and promised their lives would soon be better, even though she barely believed it herself.

In early 2008, after two long years of living in substandard housing, one of her caseworkers suggested she apply for a home through HFHSCC (Habitat for Humanity St. Charles County), near St. Louis. The word was out that Habitat was looking for a family who had lost everything in Hurricane Katrina. At first, she was excited, but soon doubted the opportunity. She feared rejection and felt there must be someone else who needed it as much as or more than she did. (Six months earlier, an unrelated agency had worked with her on a different housing opportunity that fell through, which just compounded her fears.)

Tara decided she couldn't give up and agreed to meet the people at Habitat for Humanity. The moment she walked into their office, she felt at ease and was comfortable discussing her situation. Following the interview and paperwork, the only thing left to do was to wait. Patience, out of necessity, had become one of her best virtues. She tried not to get her hopes up since she had been disappointed so many times before. She didn't yearn for extravagance. She just wanted a nice home for her family in a good neighborhood. Was that too much to want? Four months later, Tara received information that would, once again, alter the course of her life; only this time, *this* life-changing moment was a positive one, a joyful one, a miraculous one! She knew she would never look at life quite the same again.

She and her children were chosen to receive one of eight Habitat for Humanity houses to be built on a lovely cul-de-sac in a nice, family-friendly neighborhood! She could hardly believe it was true. For so long, all she had heard was, "No. Not yet. I'm sorry." But this day was different. This was a day of celebration. The promise she made to her children at the homeless shelter so long ago was actually coming true.

When the time came for work to begin on her house, Tara threw herself into the "350 Sweat Equity Hours," meaning that she, too, contributed to the building of her own home, which she considered an honor. The physical labor is part of Habitat's requirements of each home recipient. The owner must also pay a mortgage and insurance costs, contrary to widespread misconceptions about the organization's policies—one of which is that people receive a new house *for free*. Obviously, that is not true!

In August 2008, Tara and her two children, who had been through so much, moved into their new home, almost three years to the day after losing everything they once had. Those long ago possessions were no longer important to Tara, as she realized her life was continuing on just the way it was meant to.

* The above story was accepted for publication in the Kiwi Publishing anthology: *Thin Threads;*

More Real Stories of Life Changing Moments.
(2010)

Footnote #1: July 2009: Tara loves her home and her life. In addition to working full time and spending time with her children, she also teaches in a ministry and volunteers on behalf of Habitat for Humanity in St. Charles, helping others realize their dream of owning their own homes. The quote: "God's grace is sufficient" is what kept Tara going during those very difficult years.

Footnote #2: November 2012: When I knew I was getting close to finishing my memoir, I asked Tara if she would like to add another footnote about what's new in her life, and she said a resounding yes. The following are Tara's words:

"After my layoff as a St. Charles County Case Manager Coordinator in 2010, my life changed again. I applied for unemployment, made drastic financial changes, and monitored my spending more with three children. My oldest son Michael was preparing for college; Terrika was preparing for middle school; and since Malachi [adopted son] was so young, his needs were small. However, Michael and Terrika were involved with outside school events, which resulted in extra-curricular expenses. As you know with growing children, you tend to spend more money on clothes, shoes, food, necessities, allowance, etc. Not only personal expenses became great but household maintenance couldn't be neglected—bills such as cable, water, electric, Internet, car note, car and health insurance, medical, personal property tax, mortgage, etc. As the head of my household, I had to prioritize! I remember lowering my cable needs to basic, losing Internet service from time to time, and facing electric and water company disconnection notices. I look back and realize how the grace of God had to intervene because man power didn't care!

"At some point of this journey, I realized during some of my quiet days of unemployment that I needed more education. After being accepted to Lindenwood University's (St. Charles, MO) counseling program and the University of Missouri's (St. Louis, MO) education program, I became determined to build my resume. Teaching and social service has always been a realm of passion in my life. It has always been an inspiration to help people—whether through counseling or teaching. I am now close to completing my M.Ed., and it feels great! It's not easy; however, I am determined to keep it moving and perhaps start teaching in the community—and not just inside classroom walls. Meanwhile, I continue to work part time in order to make some income, as I attend the University of Missouri (UMSL) full time.

"Also my car has been paid for, and the mortgage is still my high priority. I am so thankful that my children and I have a place called home.

"Michael now attends Lindenwood's Illinois campus, and Terrika is in middle school. Malachi continues day care and comes home with so much to talk about. I must say I am a proud mama!

"Times are hard, but faith kicks in and reminds me that I made it through hard times before, and I'll make it through again. God's grace is sufficient!"

From Pigtails to Chin Hairs

The One-Chair Porch

(One of my rare attempts writing fiction.)

Most summer nights, I sit out here on my front porch trying to enjoy the evening in spite of the heat and the nasty mosquitoes. That darn candle I bought after seeing it on TV, promising it'll keep those pests away, never works for me. I light it every time I come out here, and all it does is act like a beacon. They come swarming and dive-bombing at me, like I'm the enemy in a WWII movie. How's a person supposed to enjoy themselves outdoors? I can't even relax when I'm constantly swatting my newspaper at those bloodsuckers.

It's almost unbearably hot and humid out here. I'll stay as long as I can, though. I have my glass of iced tea, and I do manage to fan myself once in a while. I also have my hanky to wipe the beads of perspiration from my face. Oooh, it feels good to sit a spell. I'm so glad I came out in time to see the sun go down, too. That's one of the prettiest sights in the whole world. It's still kind of a tradition, too, even though things are different now.

I remember summers from years past when we didn't have air conditioning. It was so miserable, especially trying to sleep in a stifling hot room. I'd be awake half the night, just turning my pillow over and over, trying to get a few seconds of the cooler side. What's that old saying about the air being so thick you could cut it with a knife?

The webbing on this old lawn chair has been fraying for a couple of summers now. It's still pretty comfortable though, so no need to spend money on a new one. Besides, it just wouldn't be the same as when there was a pair of matching chairs out here. No, I suppose I'll never get a new one. This old thing will just have to last as long as I do.

I've been working most of the day, cleaning and doing the wash like I always do on Fridays. That way I can sit and relax a bit during the weekend. Maybe a friend will stop by and visit awhile. That's another reason I like to sit out here in the evenings. Sometimes the neighbors walk their dogs along the sidewalk, look my way, and smile or wave.

It can be mighty lonesome being an old widow lady. My Fred's been gone for a few years now. He fell in an accident at his work and died right there on the spot. I didn't even get the chance to say goodbye or I love you or anything. I guess he pretty much knew all those things. Still, it would've been nice to say them, you know, one more time.

Guess I better get back inside, now that it's getting dark. Besides, I'm getting eaten alive out here. I feel those itchy bites sprouting up all over my skin. Looks like I'll be quite a sight in my blue nightgown after I get my arms and legs all polka-dotty pink with calamine lotion. Well, since there's no one here to see me, what does it matter?

I ease up slowly 'cause I'm stuck to the seat. I guess it might help if I wasn't so sweaty and flabby. I always get those funny crisscross marks on the backs of my thighs, too, from sitting here so long. It's time to blow out that useless candle and go back inside. As I open the screen door and shuffle through the doorway, I kind of whisper out loud, "I miss you, Fred. I wish you were here with me. The front porch just isn't the same without you and your chair."

Various Tiny Lights Essays

Note: I was a regular contributor to the
Searchlights & Signal Flares section of *Tiny Lights:
A Journal of Personal Narrative* from 2009 until
2012. Editor, Susan Bono posed monthly questions
that were almost unanswerable, inviting writers to
submit whatever answers they came up with. I'm
including some of my favorite responses here.

Where does your "vision" come from?   8/15/12
     Ah, another challenging question posed by the
illustrious Susan Bono.
     Since I write creative non-fiction and memoir,
my vision comes from my own memories. I don't
have to have a wild imagination to write my stories.
But those images don't automatically appear in my
mind as if they happened yesterday, last month, or
last year. They arrive from a distant time through
assorted sights, sounds, and smells. Sometimes just
hearing the first few lyrics or melody of a song
transports me to a precise moment in time.
     Example: Glenn Miller's "In the Mood." I'm
five years old and it's 1958.The 45 record drops and
spins on our heavy, wooden hi-fi. I hop onto our

scratchy gray couch and watch my parents dance in our tiny living room. I hum along, too, because I've heard it so many times. I see smiles and love and happiness. I feel happy too, and secure believing my parents will always be like this, that my life will always be like this.

Just a few short years later, though, when I hear that song, it brings jumbled feelings of hurt, anger, and sadness; because my dad has left us and I can't understand why.

Even today, more than fifty years later, I still have a few jumbled feelings, but also a new kind of vision. Forgiveness.

What does it mean to be fearless in writing?
9/15/12

I think all writers should be fearless in their writing. If they aren't, then they can't possibly be writing their best stuff, can they?

Fearless is:
Believing in yourself
Going out on a limb
Taking chances
Writing words that sometimes flow
Writing words that sometimes trickle
Forging ahead even when writer's block attacks
Fighting off self-sabotage
Staying true to your own voice

Some writers are fearless from the moment they scribble their first sentence; others may take years to feel that way, but whenever or however it happens, it's magical.

How would you describe writer's block?   12/15/10

Writer's Block makes me crazy. Writer's Block is an evil force that keeps the words locked up in my mind. I imagine myself typing all the beautiful words onto my laptop, in rapid speed with no mistakes, finishing my memoir in record time. But, no...Evil Writer's Block won't allow that and only laughs menacingly at me. That's okay. I'll play his little game....for now. I'll let him think he's preventing me from writing, but I'll have the last laugh. You see...I'm on a Christmas hiatus and hadn't planned on writing again until after the first of the year, anyway. So, take *that*, you nasty Block-Head, you! Bwahahahah.

Which is more useful to a writer, suffering or joy? 6/15/11

Oh, Susan, you really did it to me this time! The questions you pose each month are always challenging, some more so than others. Some I can respond to in a humorous way, others not so much. But this one. This one.....

I don't think there is just one answer. Haven't we all lived through suffering times? And haven't we also lived in joyous moments? Because of both emotions, that is why we write. I believe it to be especially so when writing memoir. Who wants to read an entire book of suffering? (Well, some people maybe, but not me.) And who would believe a story about a life that was incessantly joyful? I think we've realized that only happens in fairy tales.

Suffering and joy are like the salt and pepper of life. We may not *need* both ingredients, but it certainly makes life more challenging. There's that word again: challenging. YOU, Ms. Bono, are the salt and pepper of this writer's life!

What would I ask from the Writing Fairy   12/15/11

Would this Writing Fairy be able to grant any and all wishes? Similar to Samantha on *Bewitched*? Such as a simple twitch of the nose, and voilà, I'd get what I most wanted?

If that's how it worked, I wouldn't ask for a finished manuscript. I wouldn't feel as if it were my own writing if I did that. Instead, I'd ask for motivation, talent, and perseverance. I'd ask for energy to keep on going when I feel as if I'll fall asleep at my laptop. I'd ask to have faith in myself and believe that my dreams are within reach. I'd ask to enjoy the journey. Earn my success. Live the dream.

What does it mean to have a voice?   11/15/11

I've heard various explanations about what a writer's voice is, and it seems to mean different things to different people. I see it as immediately recognizing a particular writer's words once you've read something of his/hers.

John Grisham's voice comes through loud and clear; so does David Sedaris, Philip Gulley, and

Fannie Flagg. I read as much of their work as I can. I know them. They are my friends.

My first real piece of writing was published in my county's local newspaper. I wasn't trying to write like anyone else. I just wrote from my heart and the words flowed. Because of that essay, I was chosen to be one of several "guest" Opinion Shapers. (Definition: No Payment) To this day, I am grateful I was given that opportunity because it helped me hone my writing. I developed my voice.

Now, if my words would just flow every time I sat down to write, I'd have my memoir completed. I'd be working on my second book and people would definitely know who I am. They would know my voice.

What makes us forget or remember?   11/15/10

According to psychiatric studies, traumatic events can cause people to completely block out unpleasant memories. At other times, painful recollections may never go away, which can create serious problems for individuals. Whichever way you look at it, memories are very powerful.

For those of us who write creative non-fiction, personal essays, and memoirs, our memory is a huge part of who we are: It has a role in our daily lives. It's where we go every time we sit at our desk and place fingers on our laptop keys. It's our meditative place.

What makes us forget? Sometimes it's the blocking out of our sad memories. Sometimes it's our age. We can't remember the way we used to. We haven't talked about those topics in so long, they've left our mind. That must be where that expression, *I'm losing my mind* comes from! Bit by bit those memory cells begin to dry up and disappear. It's as if our mind has four seasons, and one is fall. The memories become so old, they behave like autumn leaves. They wither up and die.

But, what makes us remember? Oh, so many things, especially when the memories are happy ones! A song, a smell, a book, a movie or TV show, a tree, a holiday, a voice, a touch, a color, a piece of clothing, a flower, photographs, a memento, a certain meal, antiques, an everyday sound such as a barking dog.

One particular sound that always transports me back to my childhood is that of a prop plane. It's not very common to see or hear one flying overhead these days and I suppose that's what makes it extra special. But when I was a little girl, that's just about the only noise we heard coming from an airplane. There weren't many jet engines at that time and we lived near an aeronautical college, where small propeller planes would take off and land frequently. And because my dad was a professor there, I was deeply enamored with airplanes, and still am to this day.

Because all of my memories obviously aren't happy ones, I thrive on the ones that are. I also accept and allow the not-so-pleasant ones to have a moment of my time. I want to remember them, too. I want to remember them all, so I can get them written down and included in my memoir, before it's too late, and I've forgotten how to remember.

Where Do Memories Come From?   11/15/09

This question has bothered me ever since I read it, which was about four months ago. That's when I first came across Tiny Lights and looked at the upcoming questions. I managed to answer "What helps you remember?", so it bothers me even more that this particular, similar question has me in such a quandary!

I feel like yelling, "Where do you *think* they come from?", and then providing my own, comedic answers, which would most likely require censoring. However, I'm not about to give up without trying, so here's what I believe.

My memories come from that area in my brain which stores all the marvelous, happy moments in my life. I've realized over the years that my mind does not want to validate the hurtful and upsetting events I've tread through along this journey of mine. I've learned ways to cope and because of them, my memories are joyful, blissful, wonderful. During those rare periods when the unpleasant incidents do edge their way back into my thoughts, I'm always amazed at how quickly the sorrow and heartache can be turned back into delight, sometimes by just being grateful for my Here and Now. I know, too, that these moments I'm living now will surely be found later on, in that happy part of my brain. That's where my memories come from.

Where does your mind go when it wanders?
2/15/10

Since I am a writer, my mind constantly wanders. I have a very difficult time focusing on any one task at any given time.

Because I write non-fiction essays and memoir, my mind continually meanders from one decade to another. As it strolls along, it scratches and digs up fragments of people and events in my life, giving me enough time to jot down a few remembrances. Other times, it suddenly zigzags back and forth between the past and present, scooping up every memory and thought in its path, and dumps a mountain full of words and images at my feet.

As I attempt to gather the information and put it to some kind of useful purpose, such as in my memoir, my mind really begins to wander, and not constructively.

Did I remove that load of laundry from the washer and put it in the dryer?

Where's my grocery list? I need to add dog food to it.

What was it Ron said he needed from the pharmacy?

Okay, where was I? Oh yeah. I'm writing my book.

What is the Past Made of/Located? 6/15/10

The past is made of tiny particles, too many to count, as in our Solar System. It's the air we inhaled and exhaled, during times of happiness, or sadness, or fear.

It's made of the countless tears we shed, either heartbreaking or joyous.

It's made of the dirt we tracked into our homes after walking through grassy lawns covered with the morning dew. It's also the dirt stuck to our shoes after shuffling across a dusty ball field, while taking the short-cut home.

It's made of the distant, far off whispers of giggles and laughter that have lingered for decades near the horizon.

It's made of everything we can or cannot see, can or cannot remember, can or cannot feel. Yet it always surrounds us.

What Keeps You from Getting Stale?   8/15/2011

My writing habits are not structured and I don't follow any rules. In fact, I get a bit of a complex every time I read an article stating, "You must write every day." I've learned to skim over or entirely skip those pieces of inspiration. Growing up Catholic, I've had my fair share of self-inflicted guilt and I certainly don't want any more, especially concerning my writing.

So, what keeps me from getting stale? I haven't discovered it yet, because I do get stale. Something tells me a great number of writers experience that dreadful affliction from time to time. At least it would make me feel a lot better if they did. Come on novelists, playwrights, poets and essayists. Let's stand and unite. Stale Happens.

What Helps You Remember?   8/15/09

What helps me remember what? My name? Where I live? That I'm a writer? I am the first to admit that I have a peculiar memory when it comes to some things. I'm not talking about the usual misplaced keys, the missing remote control, or forgetting to buy milk at the grocery store. I'm talking about important events that involve family and friends.

Not too long ago, I made lunch plans with a friend and totally forgot to go. I didn't remember a thing about it until she called and I heard her voice on the phone. You can imagine how I felt and I'm sure it was noteworthy for her self-esteem, too.

Another time, a couple of girlfriends and I discussed whether to exchange Christmas gifts any longer. A few days or weeks after we'd had that conversation, I couldn't remember if I should buy presents or not. I was accused by one as having "selective memory." Huh? I don't have selective memory. Besides only children and men have that deficiency.

When it comes to my writing, though, almost anything triggers memories. Just being aware of my surroundings, just being aware of life, just living in the moment and taking it all in. On a large scale: sights, sounds, aromas, music, books, and movies. On a smaller scale: laughter, tears, meat loaf, wind chimes, lawn mowers, cinnamon rolls, crickets, chirping of birds, fizz and bubbles of carbonated drinks, cicadas, walking in snow, barking dogs, steam rising from a coffee cup, cigarette ashes barely hanging on, the glorious silence of falling snow and catching flakes on your tongue, the time traveling aroma of the pages in a book.

All of this is what makes me remember. The then and the now. I'm getting it written down as fast as I can, before I forget.

~ ~ ~

To Be Continued…..

I sincerely hope you enjoyed reading my memoir.
Please watch for the sequel coming out sometime in
2015. It will be more of the same: memories and
anecdotes from the 1950s to present day.

Thank you!

Permission Acknowledgements

Chicken Soup for the New Mom's Soul – "A Joyous Journey"
Chicken Soup for the Soul: Love Stories – "Through the Years"
Chicken Soup for the Soul: Divorce and Recovery – "Thoughts on Love and Forgiveness"
Chicken Soup for the Soul: Teens Talk....Getting Into College – "Live Your Dream"
Patchwork Path: Treasure Box – "Precious Cargo"
Thin Threads: More Real Stories of Life Changing Moments – "Habitat for Humanity"
Not Your Mother's Book...On Dogs – "Rocky Loses by a TKO"
Cuivre River Anthology Vol. V – "Piggy Back Toes & Coffee Can Spittoons"
St. Charles County (Missouri) *Journals* – various "Opinion Shaper" columns
Tiny Lights: *Searchlights & Signal Flares* www.tiny-lights.com

Adair County Free Press (Greenfield, Iowa) – "Becky's Thoughts & Observations" columns:
Freedom of Speech pg 67 ~ 3/12/08 & 9/17/08
A Timeless Journey pg57 ~ 3/26/08 & 1/7/09
That Crowbar Changed Everything pg 105 ~ 4/30 & 5/14/08
Greenfield, Mayberry, and Harmony pg 71 ~ 7/08
My Sister, My Mother, My Friend pg 175 ~ 7/9/08
Childhood Bliss in Greenfield, Iowa pg 63 ~ 8/6/08
Piggyback Toes & Coffee Can Spittoons pg 75 ~ 9/24/08
Out of the Mouths of Babes pg 219 ~ 12/31/08
The 1950s Were Almost Perfect pg 23 ~ 5/13/09
The Answer Was Right in Front of Me pg 209 ~ 6/24/09

ideas—

Blogs w/questions   last chapter
"why ... what ... How ....

pg 289

look up her other books

Made in the USA
Coppell, TX
08 September 2020